MARK TWAIN

AND THE
MAKING OF AMERICAN LITERATURE

FROM TALL TALES TO
TIMELESS CLASSICS

BLAKE WHITWORTH

Contents

Introduction

On a humid July evening in 1884, the steamboat "Gold Dust" docked along the Mississippi River, its whistle echoing through the small town of Hannibal. Mark Twain—born Samuel Clemens—stood on the deck, hat tilted back, surveying the muddy water that had shaped his boyhood. He was older now, his hair streaked with gray, but his eyes sparkled with mischief. That night, Twain lingered on Main Street, swapping stories with townsfolk, laughter ringing out over the hum of crickets. He had a gift for turning simple moments into legends, for seeing the humor and humanity in everyone he met. It was there, in the ordinary and the wild, that Twain found the roots of what would become American literature.

This book, "Mark Twain and the Making of American Literature: From Tall Tales to Timeless Classics," has a clear aim. I want to show you why Twain's work remains vital, surprising, and deeply human. Twain was more than a humorist or a spinner of tall tales. He was a sharp observer, a critic, and a friend to those forgotten by polite society. My vision is to help you see Twain as he truly was: not just a legend, but a man who shaped the way Americans tell stories and see themselves.

The central question that guides this book is simple, yet profound: How did Mark Twain become the voice of America, and what can his life and work teach us about our own? It is easy to repeat the old stories—Twain as the riverboat pilot, Twain as the wit. But behind these familiar images lies a deeper story. Twain's humor was a shield and a sword. His kindness was real, but so was his struggle with doubt and loss. How did one man's life capture the sweep of a nation's hopes and contradictions? This book will follow that question from the muddy banks of the Mississippi to the halls of literary fame.

My own journey with Twain began, as many do, with a worn copy of "The Adventures of Tom Sawyer." As a young reader, I was drawn to the humor and adventure. As I grew older, I found myself returning to Twain—not just for his stories, but for his wisdom and warmth. Over the years, I have devoted my work to helping people see classic authors in a new light. I have seen how easy it is for myths and misunderstandings to cloud our view of writers like Twain. My goal here is to clear away those clouds.

Many readers have told me they feel frustrated by Twain's books, which are either too heavy or too shallow. Some miss the man for the myth. Others find the writing dry, humorless, or stuck in the past. If you have ever felt lost trying to connect with Twain, this book is for you. I want to make Twain's world vivid and alive. You will see not just the legend, but the man—with his kindness, wit, faults, and dreams.

We will explore themes that run through all of Twain's work: the longing for freedom, the search for justice, and the power of laughter. We will look at how Twain's own life—his childhood in Missouri, his travels out West, his heartbreaks and triumphs—shaped his stories. You will meet the real people behind Tom Sawyer and Huck Finn. You will see how Twain faced the great issues of his time—race, wealth, war, and change—with courage and humor.

This book is written for anyone who loves history and literature. It is for students and teachers. It is for readers who want to move beyond the surface and find the real Twain. It is for those who seek guidance in understanding how a single writer could change the way a nation speaks, thinks, and dreams.

So I ask you: What does it mean to be an American writer? How do we find meaning in the stories of yesterday? And what can Mark Twain teach us about our own search for hope, laughter, and understanding? As you read, I invite you to reflect, to challenge, and to add your own voice to the long, rich story that Twain began so many years ago.

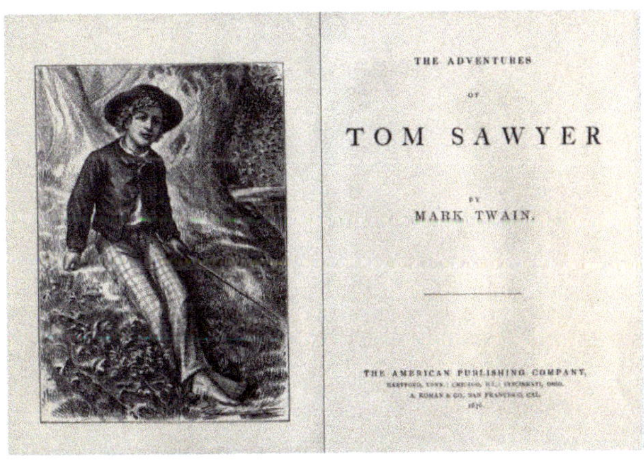

Twain's Genius: Writing the Way Americans Actually Talked

By grounding the novel in everyday speech, Twain allowed readers to experience ethical conflict as it actually occurs: hesitantly, imperfectly, in the middle of ordinary life. European novels of the period tended to showcase moral dilemmas through aristocratic drama or philosophical discourse. Twain located the American moral struggle in a raft on the Mississippi, between two outcasts searching for freedom.

This was a literary awakening. The book declared that the stories of common people—not just the rich or educated— could carry deep moral truth. It also showed that dialect, rather than diminishing seriousness, could intensify it. Huck's voice gave the novel authenticity and emotional force.

Modern writers—from Hemingway to Morrison—cite *Huck Finn* as a turning point. It expanded the boundaries of what an American novel could do and whose stories deserved to be told. Twain didn't just entertain a nation; he challenged it to examine itself in its own language.

Chapter 1: Missouri Mischief—Twain's Formative Years and the Roots of American Storytelling

Growing up in Hannibal meant living where civilization edged into wild nature. The town pressed the Mississippi's curve, its whitewashed homes perched above spring-flooded, mud-caked lanes. Woods beckoned to the west, their grapevines, fox dens, and limestone caves providing both sanctuary and mystery. The Mississippi ran as a restless force: fog drifting in, altering the landscape, each season's mood marked by adventure or danger as sandbars emerged—provocations to the town's restless youth.

Why the Mississippi River Became America's First Great Metaphor

Long before Mark Twain became a household name, he was simply Samuel Clemens, a boy staring at the endless bends of the Mississippi River. That river shaped him in ways no classroom could. It taught him patience, attentiveness, humility, and respect for power—qualities that would later seep directly into his writing. More than scenery, the Mississippi became a metaphor for the American soul.

The river was not a straight path, and neither was the country. It twisted, meandered, rose, fell, flooded, destroyed, nourished. Twain saw the beauty and the danger. He understood that life, like the river, is never still. This sensibility informed his sentences, which often drifted gently across the page before gathering momentum and hitting the reader with sudden force. That rhythm—slow, deliberate, then explosive—became one of the hallmarks of American prose.

As Twain matured, he came to realize that the Mississippi carried with it the entire nation's history: the movement of goods, the mixing of languages, the friction of cultures. On its waters floated the voices of preachers, gamblers, enslaved people, freedmen, immigrants, and restless adventurers. The river was America talking. And Twain, attentive as always, was listening.

When he wrote *Life on the Mississippi* and later *Huckleberry Finn*, he transformed the river from a real place into a symbolic one. For readers, the Mississippi became a road of possibility—dangerous, unpredictable, and full of moral choices. Huck and Jim drift on their current, not toward adventure alone, but toward the question at the heart of the American conscience: Who are we, and who do we want to become?

Modern critics often call the Mississippi "Twain's greatest character." They aren't wrong. The river reflects his belief that American identity is fluid, evolving, and endlessly complex. It mirrors the nation's hopes and contradictions. And even now, long after riverboats have disappeared from daily life, the Mississippi continues to define Twain's place in American literature: a writer who understood that the story of a nation can be read not only in its laws and institutions, but in the movement of its people and the language of its waters.

Hannibal Roots—Childhood Along the Mississippi

Twain's early years unfolded in this vibrant setting, providing sound, color, and memory woven into his later prose. The busy riverfront was a corridor for goods and strangers from far cities. Main Street was alive with hammering, laughter, and vendors peddling wares, mingled with smells of manure, honeysuckle, frying catfish, and tobacco. Evenings glowed with lamp light and frog choruses.

Nature was ever-present. Sam and friends explored woods, wandered creeks, and ventured into shadowy caves. Summers brought heavy heat and sudden storms; winters, swirling snow confined families, who swapped stories by firelight.

Hannibal's residents were a mosaic: Black and white, slave and free, Irish, German, and itinerant river men. Twain's family lingered on the edge of poverty—his father's schemes rarely working out, though his mother brought warmth and stories (see: How Mark Twain's Childhood Influenced His Literary Works). Amid neighbors of varied backgrounds, Sam honed his listening, eavesdropping on dialects unfiltered by print.

Town personalities later became Twain's characters. Huck owed much to Tom Blankenship, the freedom-loving son of a local drunk. Aunt Polly was shaped by caring, strict matriarchs of Hill Street. Enslaved people like Uncle Daniel, who told stories by firelight, taught young Sam about endurance. Dockworkers—Black men unloading cargo, Irishmen mending nets—shared rumors and news. Such characters embroidered the world that Twain later depicted in fiction.

River life sparked more than imagination—it bred skepticism. Steamboat disasters like the one that killed Twain's brother, Henry, shaped his early worldview (How Mark Twain's Childhood Influenced His Literary Works). Hannibal faced epidemics: yellow fever, malaria could upend life overnight. Floods erased streets. Superstition flourished: charms traded, ghost tales told, black cats avoided. These beliefs colored young Twain's world.

Peril fueled dreams of escape. The river beckoned—risk and liberation in equal parts. Boys dreamed of being pirates or finding buried treasure. Twain's tales regularly featured characters breaking free of family, poverty, or social restriction.

The Mississippi soon became a recurring symbol for Twain—serene, treacherous, yet always promising. In "Huckleberry Finn," Huck and Jim flee injustice, the raft becoming their refuge. Even as a child, Twain saw how class and race shaped freedom and invisibility.

Whitewashing the Fence—The Real Stories Behind Tom Sawyer's Mischief

Before Tom Sawyer won literary fame, young Sam Clemens stood sweating beside a fence that stretched unendingly—a punishment for mischief. Yet, instead of complaining, he flipped the situation. With quick banter, Sam persuaded others that fence-painting was desirable, letting them line up with marbles and apples for his brush, while he rested in the shade. Twain later transformed this into The Adventures of Tom Sawyer's enduring whitewashing scene, admitting he only painted a strip of the real Hill Street fence. Fact exaggerated by comedy became fiction's gold.

Sam's boyhood mischief wasn't isolated. His gang of local boys thrived on wild schemes—hunting for treasure, staging mock robberies, and playing pirates on nearby islands. Adults rarely intervened, and imagination reigned. Once, the boys faked their deaths on Jackson's Island, returning at their own "funeral" to shock townfolk. In Sunday School, Sam connived his way to a Bible prize by trading trinkets for colored verse tickets, a scheme exposed under the minister's scrutiny.

Twain's brilliance lay in transforming small events into shining narrative moments. He inflated everyday pranks with vivid exaggeration, timing, and wit. In the fence scene, awe, Tom's fake reluctance, and a growing heap of treasures elevate a simple task. Mischief, under Twain's hand, revealed intelligence and innocence, never crossing into malice.

Mischief framed Twain's examination of Hannibal's youthful social codes: the rules, status, and subtle power struggles. Obedience was valued, both at home and church, but rebellion smoldered. Chores were punishments. Sunday School tickets conferred status. Pranks became acts of peer-powered rebellion, letting children gain respect without adult mediation. Twain understood: even in games, children grapple with authority.

Behind these playful rebellions lay more than fun—there was subversive critique. Tom's boundary-testing tricks mirrored Twain's own doubts about blind obedience. The fence scene isn't just funny—it's slyly rebellious; Tom profits from punishment by stirring up the ambitions of others, showing how easily rules can be bent with convincing talk.

These lessons in subversion matured into Twain's later satire. Mischief became a metaphor for examining and upending convention—using wit against hypocrisy or arbitrary authority. Later, "Huckleberry Finn" advanced this rebellion: Huck's disobedience emerges as an act of both cleverness and conscience. Twain saw in every youthful prank a subtle protest against social lies and hypocrisy.

Even today, Tom Sawyer's adventures resonate as more than nostalgia. They reveal how children claim agency within restrictive worlds—bending rules to find freedom and self-knowledge. Twain's stories remind us: even minor acts of mischief can reflect larger truths, using humor and imagination to claim independent space amidst pressure to conform.

Slave Narratives and Neighborly Voices—Forming Twain's Dialect Dialogue

Hannibal evenings ended by hearths or near slave quarters, where stories flowed like currents. Young Sam Clemens listened raptly to the town's Black residents' tales—stories of loss, cunning heroes, haunted woods, escapes—rich in sorrow, wit, and resilience. Their oral traditions shaped Twain profoundly: he absorbed not just the sound but the survival, wit, and wisdom in every syllable. In these circles, language wasn't style—it was identity and resistance.

Twain's ear for authentic speech sharpened early, tuned by myriad voices. His mother's gentle twang, a neighbor's Irish accent, river hands' concise chatter, and enslaved workers' blend of African American Vernacular, slang, and proverbs—he internalized the underlying grammar, rhythm, and meaning. Later, as he voiced Jim or Huck, he wove these models carefully, selecting phrasing for authentic effect.

What separated Twain's dialogue was his refusal to sanitize. While most American novels favored 'correct' English, Twain let characters speak truly. "I'm rich now," grumbles Jim; "I lit out," says Huck. Such lines startled readers used to formality. His prose pulsed with n-grams, contractions, and repeated turns—giving fiction the unpredictability of real talk. This democratized voice let even those marginalized by society speak for themselves.

Yet, Twain's work is not without modern controversy. His use of Black dialect—especially Jim's—has drawn criticism: sometimes reinforcing racial stereotypes or ignorance. Some argue his intentions were admirable, his aim being authenticity and humanization of the dehumanized. Twain himself wanted to capture lived speech, not textbook ideals. Still, the debate endures, especially around "Injun Joe," whose portrayal sometimes slipped from empathy into damaging cliché.

In these moments, Twain's dialect is shielded and spotlighted. It offers resistance, jokes, and sharp insights into moral and social complexity. For today's readers, these passages ask uncomfortable questions about language's power—to harm, to stereotype, and to reveal. Twain knew every voice mattered—he challenged literature to not just sound, but listen.

Twain and the Rise of American Individualism

Few writers embodied the American spirit of individualism more powerfully than Mark Twain. He admired rebels, nonconformists, dreamers, and wanderers—people who stepped outside rigid social boundaries and dared to think for themselves. This admiration shaped not only his character but the very way he believed Americans should speak and write.

"The Frontier as a Linguistic Laboratory"

Twain did not invent American English, but the frontier created the conditions where it could finally breathe. The rivers, mining camps, wagon trails, and rough settlements of the 19th-century West were linguistic melting pots. People from the East mingled with immigrants from Europe, freedmen, Native Americans, and adventurers from every social level. Words collided, blended, and changed shape. Twain captured this in real time. The frontier taught Twain that language is never finished. It grows, shifts, and mutates depending on who speaks it. The "American sound" he recorded was not born in elegant drawing rooms—it was forged in cabins, camps, and cookfires.

Twain grew up in a country that was still defining itself. The Civil War tore through the old order and left the nation searching for new voices and new identities. Twain's answer to this uncertainty was simple: speak honestly, even if the truth is messy. His characters rarely sound alike because real people rarely sound alike. He celebrated individuality in language, portraying speech as an extension of personality rather than a variable to be standardized.

The frontier sharpened this belief. Life in the West rewarded ingenuity and punished pretense. A river pilot or miner had to rely on instincts, not etiquette. The directness of frontier speech—blunt, humorous, sometimes crude— captured a spirit of independence that resonated with Twain. He saw authenticity as a virtue, and he despised anything that smelled of self-importance or conformity.

This reverence for individuality seeped into his writing. Tom Sawyer's mischief, Huck Finn's moral awakening, the boastfulness of the tall-tale teller, the earnestness of Jim—all stand as portraits of people refusing to be shaped by others' expectations. Even Twain's nonfiction reveals a man who valued personal freedom: his travel writings mock social rituals, his lectures skewer hypocrisy, and his essays champion independent thought.

Twain's embrace of individualism also helped define the national voice. American writing became more flexible, informal, and personality-driven in part because Twain encouraged writers to trust their own natural speech patterns. He showed that authenticity mattered more than correctness, and that a writer's voice should sound like no one else's.

In celebrating individuality, Twain offered Americans a model for how to speak, write, and even live. His legacy is not just literary—it is cultural. He taught the nation that being uniquely oneself is not a flaw but a defining feature of American identity.

Twain's personal letters reveal a man who swung between exuberance and melancholy. He could entertain thousands from the stage, but often felt alone afterward. Fame brought financial security, but did not shield him from loss. Yet through all the grief, Twain continued to write, driven by a belief that humor could connect people, soften suffering, and reveal truth.

Many authors before Twain tried to represent dialect, but most exaggerated it or forced it. Twain respected it. His characters speak with contractions, shortcuts, and regional flourishes that readers recognized instantly as authentic. This wasn't laziness; it was precision. Twain understood the physics of speech—how people interrupt themselves, how they stall, how they dodge questions, how they soften blows with humor. By recording such nuances, he didn't just capture conversation; he shaped what future writers believed dialogue could accomplish. Today's modern novelistic dialogue—casual, clipped, natural—traces its inheritance directly to Twain's experiments.

Twain's School of Hard Knocks—Early Loss, Poverty, and Resilience

Samuel Clemens's youth was shadowed by loss and need. Three siblings died in childhood. The steamboat accident that killed his brother, Henry, scarred Twain for life. His father, John, ambitious but unlucky, died of pneumonia when Sam was eleven, leaving only debts (see: How Mark Twain's Childhood Influenced His Literary Works). Malaria sickened Sam repeatedly, and the family was often forced to move, relying on neighbors' charity. Though common in antebellum Missouri, for Twain, hardship was formative, forging both resilience and skepticism.

Poverty shaped Sam's ambitions. Survival meant working where possible—from printer's apprentice (sweeping floors, setting type by hand) to reporting for his brother Orion's paper. These jobs—long, dirty, but formative— taught him the power of words and offered glimpses of escape. He dreamed of wealth—first as a river pilot, later searching for silver in the West—driven by the precariousness of fortune.

Hardship grew Twain's compassion. He saw fortunes rise and fall, families split by misfortune, and good luck reversed overnight. Twain came to trust grit and wit over pedigree. Befriending outcasts, he preferred figures who defied societal rules. This outsider perspective fueled the rebelliousness running through his fiction—characters who refused to submit to authority for its own sake.

Humor was his shield. Laughter made hunger, grief, or disappointment bearable. Twain wrote: "Humor is mankind's greatest blessing"—a thread running through all his stories. Even tragedy became tinged with sly hope. Not naive, nor despairing, Twain's worldview became one of endurance: skeptical but never crushed.

These experiences appear in his fiction's recurring motifs: resilience, reinvention, orphans, and outsiders surviving by wit, not tradition. Huck drifts parentless; Tom's recklessness is self-sufficiency. These are survivors—skeptics who break rules, mock pretension, and expose hypocrisy, crafting families or meaning wherever possible.

To clarify, consider a modern counterpart: a teen working weekends to support the family. The money pays for rent or groceries. These hardships foster practical wisdom, humor in difficulty, and suspicion toward those offering easy help. Twain's own childhood, much the same, shaped his ambitions and respect for the truly resourceful.

How Mark Twain Turned Ordinary Speech Into Literary Gold

When Mark Twain arrived on the literary scene, American fiction still wore a British accent. Novelists clung to elegant phrasing, formal constructions, and a tone that suggested their books belonged in parlors lined with velvet drapes. What Twain did—almost casually—was kick open the windows and let in the breeze. He wrote the way everyday Americans actually talked.

This was revolutionary. For centuries, literature had been something lofty, aspirational, and remote. Twain brought it down to the front porch. His dialogue was alive: people stammered, contradicted themselves, used slang, and said things that would have horrified a Victorian grammarian. Critics at the time even accused him of "lowering the American tongue." Yet that lowering was, in truth, a liberation. Twain recognized that authenticity lives in the ordinary rhythms of speech, not in artificially polished sentences.

And so he listened—really listened. On riverboats, in frontier towns, in mining camps, at newspaper offices, and in the smoke-filled rooms of political meetings, he absorbed voices. He wrote down idioms, turns of phrase, cadences, and peculiarities. He understood that the American language wasn't one language at all, but a quilt stitched from dialects, cultures, and experiences. His genius was not in inventing these voices, but in honoring them.

The Adventures of Huckleberry Finn became the defining example. Here was a novel that dared to use dialect not as decoration, but as truth. Huck's words were his character; Jim's language carried his pain, his humor, and his dignity. Twain did not flatten their speech into a single "proper" English—he let it stand as it was, regional, imperfect, and full of life.

In doing so, Twain changed American literature forever. He taught generations of writers that the nation's true voice was not found in imported rules or aristocratic customs, but in the everyday language spoken by millions—raw, inconsistent, musical, and unmistakably American.

At its core, Twain's humor functioned as a mirror. By exaggerating the foolishness of politicians, preachers, and pompous elites, he allowed readers to recognize their own blind spots. Yet he never positioned himself above the joke. When Twain mocked vanity or ignorance, he usually included himself in the reflection. That self-deprecating charm made his satire feel friendly rather than cruel, even when it struck painful truths.

His style of humor—deadpan, ironic, sly, and occasionally outrageous—was distinctly American. It echoed the frontier tall tale, in which ordinary people told extraordinary lies with straight faces. It borrowed from riverboat banter, where timing was everything. It drew from the country's democratic spirit, poking fun at anyone who pretended to be more important than anyone else.

Twain's humor also served as a shield. When grief overwhelmed him, when financial troubles mounted, when the losses of his wife and children nearly broke his spirit, he often retreated into jokes. Laughter became a way to manage sorrow without surrendering to it. Many of Twain's funniest pieces were written during the darkest s of his life—a fact that surprises readers but not writers, who understand the emotional alchemy humor requires.

Most importantly, Twain's humor was a weapon against injustice. His comedic critiques of racism, greed, violence, and cruelty were sharper than any sermon. He made readers laugh first and think later, which allowed uncomfortable truths to slip past their defenses. And once the truth settled in, it stayed.

Today's American humor—from satire to late-night monologues to political cartoons—still owes much to Twain's approach. He demonstrated that comedy could speak boldly, challenge authority, and illuminate the human condition. In that sense, Twain didn't just write jokes. He gave America its comedic conscience.

Twain the Reluctant Linguist: How He Preserved Voices Without Meaning To

Mark Twain never called himself a linguist, and he would have laughed at the suggestion. Yet few individuals have contributed more to the preservation of American speech. Living in a century before audio recording, Twain captured dialects, cadences, idioms, and vocal rhythms that otherwise would have vanished into history. His novels, letters, and essays form one of the richest linguistic archives of 19th-century America.

Twain did not approach language scientifically. He approached it emotionally. He wrote down what moved him, amused him, surprised him, or struck him as true. But what seems casual to modern readers was actually invaluable. In an age of rapid migration, regional dialects were evolving or disappearing, and many were never documented. Twain's ear for speech was so accurate that modern linguists still study his texts to reconstruct lost pronunciation patterns and regional distinctions.

Consider his use of seven distinct dialects in *Huckleberry Finn*. Each reflects a different social group or geographic region—from the Missouri Negro dialect to the Pike County speech patterns. Twain did not homogenize these voices, nor did he simplify them for readers. He insisted that the music of local speech mattered, even if it required effort to understand. In doing so, he made a radical assertion: every voice, no matter how marginalized, belonged in American literature.

Twain also preserved humor through language. Many of his tall tales and anecdotes rely on the peculiarities of frontier slang—phrases like "ornery," "skedaddle," "rip-snorter," and "light out." These expressions carried a cultural context that would be lost without Twain's ear and pen. Through him, we gain a glimpse of how ordinary Americans expressed frustration, joy, caution, impatience, and mischief.

In preserving these voices, Twain helped define America's identity as a nation of many tongues. His writing reminds us that language is not just a tool for communication—it is a record of who we are and where we've been. And the great irony is that this preservation was not a scholarly mission. Twain simply listened well, wrote honestly, and trusted the power of the spoken word. The result is a linguistic treasure that continues to shape American literature.

The Moral Weight of Huck Finn: Why Twain Changed the American Novel

When *The Adventures of Huckleberry Finn* appeared in 1885, critics didn't know what to do with it. Was it a children's book? A satire? A travelogue? A social commentary? It was all of these and none of them. Twain had created something unprecedented: an American novel with a moral core that emerged not from grand speeches or noble heroes but from the conscience of a barefoot boy drifting down a river.

What made the book revolutionary was its honesty. Huck does not speak in polished prose or repeat the moral lessons adults have drilled into him. Instead, he wrestles with right and wrong in the only language he knows—plain, unvarnished, struggling speech. His decision to help Jim, even when he believes it will "send him to hell," remains one of the most moving moments in American literature. Twain understood that morality is not inherited; it is chosen, and sometimes chosen in defiance of society's expectations.

Missouri's Feuds and Follies—Seeds of Satire in a Divided America

Twain's Missouri childhood was marked by contradiction—comedy and tragedy tangled. Antebellum tensions made the town square a stage for feuds and absurdity. Hannibal's local quarrels—property disputes, debts, slights—would occasionally flare into violence or prolonged grudges, inspiring the epic Grangerford-Shepherdson rivalry in "Huck Finn," where families war senselessly, the original insult long forgotten.

Small-town politics were dramatic: elections became carnivals of persuasion—candidates bribed with whiskey and pies, town meetings descended into argument or sometimes brawl. Twain watched decency dissolve under political ambition, as ministers or merchants revealed their foibles. Public virtue often doubled as performance: sermons thundered on Sundays, deals whispered in saloons on Mondays. The spectacle was both a delight and a warning for Twain.

Mob justice often replaced courts. Twain witnessed how crowds could turn violent—lynchings, duels spawned from words, whole mobs driven by rumor. Collective energy, both frightening and fascinating, etched into his mind the peril of mass emotions. "Huck Finn" depicts this bluntly: when townsfolk threaten to tar and feather the King and Duke or Colonel Sherburn, Twain unmasks mob cowardice.

His moral surroundings were unstable—piety lived beside vice, with church bells chiming over gambling dens. Ministers led both sermons and scandals, and charity often disguised apathy. Twain's eye for hypocrisy sharpened early; he distrusted grand claims and favored subtle skepticism, learning that virtue loudly proclaimed was often least reliable.

Violence underpinned daily life—children grew used to gunshots and arguments. Twain realized that survival required wit and humor as much as obedience. The tall tale—stories spun higher and madder—helped process uncertainty, using exaggeration to mask or deflate anxiety.

Humor was more than an escape—it was a weapon. Twain learned that laughter skewered arrogance more effectively than confrontation. Through mockery, he exposed pretense, revealed abuse of power, and let the powerless reclaim some agency.

Twain's satire cut deepest in depicting mob folly. He skewered collective abandon, showing how quickly sense evaporates. In "Huck Finn," Sherburn confronts a mob, mocking their supposed bravery—they scatter when faced with real danger.

Missouri's contradictions—violence beside faith, comedy with cruelty—shaped Twain's outlook indelibly. Justice was never blind, and decency needed vigilant defense. Rather than cynicism, Twain found comic perspective: storytelling could expose pretense and bring light to society's darkest corners.

The tall tale, with its exaggerations and wit, became Twain's means of ordering chaos. Humor let him process what might feel overwhelming—turning confusion into a story, risk into something bearable. This attitude— questioning crowds and those claiming authority— underpinned everything he wrote.

The First Tall Tales—Anecdotes, Yarn-Spinning, and the Birth of a Storyteller

After supper, Sam Clemens gathered under lamplight or the moon, listening to Hannibal's riverfront storytellers. The river brought not just goods but legends, jokes, and laughter. Fishermen spun yarns of giant catfish and narrow escapes. Traveling showmen boasted impossible feats. Fireside tales grew with each retelling—accuracy mattered less than suspense or a good punchline. Sam noticed how men exaggerated, fostering excitement and disbelief, and soon learning the value of pacing and comic timing.

This storytelling culture deeply influenced young Sam. He began imitating local tales, making up his own with humor and exaggeration—like the "ghost dog" in the graveyard, or the fisherman tricked by a submerged log. "Truth" was fluid—tales were meant to marvel and tease, not merely inform.

Practical jokes further honed Sam's flair for performance. He fooled siblings with fake treasure hunts or staged attic "snake scares." His antics delighted friends, sometimes trying teachers' patience, but always focused on laughter, never harm. These mischiefs taught him about audience: how to engage, when to deliver the twist, and the importance of the storyteller's wink—a signal to take tales with a grain of salt.

That "wink"—not taking stories too seriously—became Twain's literary signature, especially in satirical works. He relished keeping listeners guessing, mixing truth and fiction, delighting in the tension of ambiguity.

Risk-taking, dares, and jokes defined Twain's boyhood. He often challenged others to swim across the river or join nighttime adventures; this taught him that daring (be it physical or social) could yield both risk and reward. These instincts, honed through playful bets and escapades, later shaped his broader narrative style.

These formative years—the tall tales, jokes, and performance—eventually culminated in Twain's first popular story, "The Celebrated Jumping Frog of Calaveras County." Its humor stemmed not only from absurd circumstances but also from the deadpan narration and expectancy-managing delivery. Readers entered worlds where logic twisted, and gullibility was fair game. That sly authorial wink let readers in on the joke—a trait central to Twain's enduring charm.

For Twain, humor served not just to amuse but to survive hardship, challenge pomposity, and defuse risk. Mastering the art of storytelling, he found his authorial voice—a blend of mischief, resilience, and keen observation. Twain's tale-spinning roots remind us: storytelling is shared performance—connecting people, inviting laughter, and revealing human truths.

The musicality, slyness, and spirit that define Twain's masterpieces all grew from those lively nights in Hannibal. The watchful boy by the fire ultimately became America's great humorist—his tales, like the Mississippi, flowing beyond place and time, inviting new generations to join in the adventure and laughter.

Twain's fiction never romanticizes adversity. Instead, it shows struggle in forging humor, character, and new beginnings. His protagonists are rebellious but enduring, their cleverness and hope mirroring his own path—a boy battered by loss yet capable of laughter and empathy.

In stories where orphans find belonging among friends or on the river, Twain voices the hope that endurance and humor can transmute even dark circumstances into new opportunities. His own history attests to the truth: hard times don't preclude invention, connection, or eventual success.

Chapter 2 : Riverboat Gambler— Travel, Transformation, and Twain's American Identity

Steamboat Gothic—Navigating the Mississippi's Perils and Promises

Picture piloting a Mississippi steamboat at midnight, fog closing in, relying only on memory and instinct. This was Mark Twain's reality—at twenty-one, not yet famous, he stood in the pilothouse, responsible for lives and cargo. The unpredictable river was constantly reshaped by storms and shifting sandbars. Twain's training required more than skill; it demanded vigilance. Beneath calm waters lurked sunken logs, sudden shoals, and churning eddies. Piloting meant studying the river like a face, searching for the faintest clues in its motion. On foggy nights, the river became a maze. Twain and his fellow pilots kept evolving mental maps of bends, islands, and currents, sharpened by each trip. Any error invites disaster. Night shifts required total focus— heart racing as you peered into blackness, alert to distant noises and the engine's pulse. The stress was both exhilarating and frightening; it built the resilience and wit that later defined Twain's style.

Learning the river meant adapting to constant change. The Mississippi transformed daily banks fell, sandbars shifted, landmarks disappeared. Pilots memorized hundreds of miles of restless terrain. Twain wrote, "the face of the water...became a wonderful book—a dead language to the uneducated, but which told its mind to me." The river, in Twain's eyes, was more than a backdrop; it was a dynamic, untamed protagonist, both fickle and formidable.

In "Life on the Mississippi," Twain makes the river itself central—steering fates, upending plans, gentle and then treacherous. The river entices with freedom—tempting Huck and Jim to escape and adventure—but is always perilous, demanding respect. In "Adventures of Huckleberry Finn," the river shapes Huck and Jim's journey; every twist brings new tests and unexpected lessons. Their raft is a floating refuge, away from society, birthing unlikely friendship and new rules. Yet safety is temporary; threats from steamboats and slave catchers persist, reminding us freedom often comes shadowed by risk.

Steamboat culture had its own order—strict yet lively, fierce, and forged by shared perils. Pilots reigned as kings; their expertise went unquestioned by captains and owners, as only they grasped the river's secrets. Rivalries thrived— pilots jealously guarded knowledge of hidden channels. Newcomers had to prove themselves, facing silent tests, wary glances, and even sabotage. But cramped quarters built camaraderie: shared meals, late-night stories, deep bonds, and mutual wariness of authority.

Superstitions flourished onboard. Crew refused to whistle below deck—fearing storms—or launch on Fridays. Unwritten codes shaped everything from greetings to storytelling, which Twain eagerly absorbed for later comedic or critical use.

Danger was constant. Boiler explosions shattered nights; hidden wrecks spun boats off course. Twain himself narrowly survived the Pennsylvania steamboat boiler explosion, which killed several—among them his brother Henry—a tragedy haunting him with guilt and highlighting life's unpredictability. This turmoil fed Twain's dark humor: jokes about death around every bend, tales of pilots vanishing overnight.

The river's demand for constant attention brought renewal—each dawn offered a new opportunity; every setback, resilience, and humility. For Twain, the mixture of peril and promise shaped not just his piloting, but his vision as an American writer. The river's restless, shifting spirit became entwined with his identity and art.

The Language of the River—Crafting Authentic American Voices

Life on the Mississippi surrounded Twain with countless voices—loud, quiet, each carrying a story. Deckhands swapped tall tales in rough blends of Irish, German, and Deep South dialects. Traders haggled in practical, clipped speech; passengers from cities brought accents hinting at old money or distant roots. Pilots spoke an intricate code—terms like "towhead," "snag," "crossing," and "bar" were cryptic to outsiders but full of meaning to insiders. Twain listened intently, learning that words, tone, and timing signified class, intent, and even insult. The river, a crossroads for language, saw dialects fuse and evolve daily.

Twain embedded these sounds into his writing, setting new standards for authenticity. In "Life on the Mississippi," he offered readers a glossary of river terms, drawing them into the pilots' world. This linguistic attention made his work vivid, as if readers stood in the pilothouse amid the shouts and smoke. Twain laced his stories with the river's rough poetry: "stage plank," "mark twain" (two fathoms), "texas deck," "larboard," "hurricane roof." These idioms rooted his fiction in the American landscape. In "Huckleberry Finn," he built characters through their speech. Huck's drawl—direct and imperfect—contrasted with Jim's gentle rhythms and the clipped talk of the raft-dwellers. Twain's dialogue did more than mimic; it revealed character, class, and prejudice.

Twain used speech to signal belonging. Awkward attempts at river slang exposed outsiders, while a pilot's mastery of technical terms commanded approval. He played with these distinctions, creating tension and humor. In "Life on the Mississippi," pilots exchange dense jargon, unintelligible to others but clear to those in the know—subtle signals establishing trust and status.

He also broke convention. Contemporary American literature often favored polished, European-style narration. Twain rebelled, refusing to smooth his characters' voices. Some critics fumed; readers, in contrast, recognized echoes of their own communities. Twain's ear for patterns—n-grams, repeated phrases—lent his dialogue authenticity. Words like "reckon," "ain't," and "by and by" recur throughout Huck's speech, rooting the novels in their time and place.

The river provided endless moments for comic misunderstanding. Passengers stumbled over pilot jargon; deckhands from distant states quarreled over word meanings. In one scene, Huck's explanations to the feuding Grangerfords are twisted by their habits and biases. Such moments aren't just jokes—they show how language can unite, divide, and confuse in equal measure.

Language, Twain understood, moved the plot as much as action. When Huck and Jim meet strangers, survival depends on quick wits—and fluency, or at least an ability to fake it. River slang becomes a protective disguise; pilot-talk warns of oncoming disaster, a single missed word sometimes spelling catastrophe.

Twain's focus on language sharpened his satire. Accents and idioms created invisible boundaries—friend from foe, insider from outsider. He exposed snobbery among educated passengers who looked down on crews they couldn't understand. Sometimes he let words betray their speakers' claims to authority. His approach was radical, then and now. Twain proved that American voices—rough-edged and polyglot, funny and biting—belonged in serious literature, unapologetically. The result: a chorus of American voices, still alive page after page.

Gambling, Risk, and Loss—The Making of Twain's Deadpan Wit

River life was a balancing act, nowhere clearer than in the card rooms and casinos below deck. Twain frequented these smoky spaces, where pilots and crews gamed to chase fortune or quell boredom, betting silver and telling stories between hands. The games weren't genteel; they were contests of nerve, bluff, and calculation. Laughter mixed with tension—everyone knew luck could turn instantly. Twain played often, sometimes losing more than he could afford. Winnings bought boots or meals; losses left you begging for your next wage. Gambling offered both amusement and training. Twain learned to read faces, habits, and sense when luck would shift. This constant risk demanded a calm exterior; betraying nerves cost dearly.

The whole rhythm of river life echoed this unpredictability. The best pilot could lose his vessel to unseen dangers, while the most reckless gambler sometimes left a winner. Twain grew philosophical—a mix of hope and cynicism. His fiction pulses with this sense of fate: in "The Notorious Jumping Frog of Calaveras County," luck dupes the hopeful and the sly alike, fortunes changing on a frog's jump or a clever trick. Twain's characters battle forces they can't master—cards, storms, chance meetings with con men. They adapt, hope, and scheme, but rarely control their fates.

This culture shaped Twain's signature humor: the deadpan. He honed it both at the wheel and at cards, telling wild stories or recounting disaster with a straight face. The graver the tale, the flatter his delivery—heightening the absurdity. Twain described epic losses and near-misses with equal calm, coaxing laughter that revealed human stubbornness against fate. From this period came memorable anecdotes—losing all at cards, then "improving in prudence by watching others lose." Every joke was layered: at once a sympathetic and sly commentary on the folly of outsmarting fortune.

Twain's river stories reveal the foundation of his later gambles—leaving a respected job as a pilot for the uncertain path of writer was itself a wager. He long understood art and business as games of chance. Later, Twain speculated wildly—investing in inventions and publishing schemes, losing fortunes, and rebuilding with lecturing and new books. These setbacks added depth to his humor—a self-mockery and acceptance of life's swings.

The river taught Twain lessons on risk that shaped his writing and characters: card games sharpened his judgment, losses bred humility and resilience. Huck Finn bets freedom on every move, Jim takes risks for dignity, and Tom Sawyer dreams up wild plans. Twain's characters expect no guarantees but face setbacks with inventiveness and wit, echoing his own attitude toward chance.

Twain's deadpan is not just for laughs—it's a shield against disappointment, a way to process life's absurdities. The river gave him a ringside seat for observing hope and hubris, fortune and loss. His unique mix of risk and cool observation stands him apart—not just an entertainer, but a keen observer of America's restless spirit.

Gold Rush Dreams—Twain's Western Adventures and Literary Breakthroughs

When Twain boarded a stagecoach for the Nevada Territory in 1861, he carried hopes for quick fortune and reinvention.

The Civil War had crippled river commerce, and Western silver strikes beckoned with new opportunities. The journey west tested patience and resolve. Roads wound through barren country, where passengers swapped stories—some true, most pure bravado—about riches and ruin. Twain was alternately awed and skeptical: the desert held stark beauty, but boomtowns teemed with chaos. Aurora, where Twain sought his fortune as a miner, offered mostly hardship; he toiled for little reward, optimism eroded by hunger and long winters. Twain saw men gamble everything on rumors—most lost, but a few endured on stories alone.

Virginia City became his crucible. The town vibrated with lawlessness—gamblers, barkeeps, sharp-eyed women read men the way others read cards. Here, Twain watched human nature unvarnished: justice decided by mob, fortunes made or lost in hours. He encountered charming con men, gamblers risking everything before breakfast, miners hooked on rumor and chance. Twain's skepticism sharpened; he learned to spot deceit beneath surfaces, his satire growing shrewder with each encounter. The West was a place of self-invention: names changed, identities recast; survival depended on wit over power.

Failing as a miner, Twain found his footing at the Territorial Enterprise, trading pick for pen but keeping his taste for risk. Reporting meant chasing stories from saloon to camp, sometimes dodging those he lampooned. He covered duels, disasters, and political feuds, often exaggerating for comic effect. Twain discovered humor was sharper than outrage readers, anxious for escape, devoured his playful sketches. Soon, public lectures followed, where Twain transformed setbacks into suspenseful, crowd-pleasing performances.

The Western landscape imprinted itself on Twain's work: deserts shimmering with heat, jagged peaks, winds flattening camps overnight. He captured this world's harsh beauty and its indifference to ambition. Mules traced lines across the horizon; miners cursed at dry pans or celebrated rare finds with reckless generosity. Twain mocked boosterism—the habit of calling every new camp "the next great city." He lampooned newspapers that exaggerated population and proclaimed every event historic.

He borrowed Western storytelling—tall tales by fireside, comic anecdotes told in crowded bars—blending exaggeration with keen observation. The West taught Twain that Americans craved stories promising transformation but knew luck often failed, and heroes were rarely pure.

In these fierce years, Twain balanced hope with skepticism. The West supplied not only material but a method: doubt grand claims, laugh at failure, never trust a supposed gold mine without seeing calluses. This period forged the Twain who emerges in his masterpieces—irreverent, searching for truth within chaos and contradiction.

Roughing It—Satire, Survival, and Self-Invention in Nevada and California

Twain's years in Nevada and California surpassed even river life's demands. The West required adaptability, wit, and sheer endurance. In Virginia City, Twain relied as much on jokes as on luck, sometimes going days on soda crackers and coffee. These hardships sharpened his humor—fewer punchlines, more ironic reflection, and resilience. Twain's pen became a survival tool, a means for self-invention. He exaggerated stories as armor, not vanity—"Roughing It" exposes Western glamour's underbelly, revealing grit behind the legend. Often, he played the clownish outsider in his tales, blundering through scams and miseries but always escaping with humor.

The voice in "Roughing It" was both disguise and confession. Twain depicted himself as naive, but his storytelling was shrewd—using exaggeration to draw laughter, slyly inviting readers into the joke. His lectures drew crowds eager to see their misfortunes lampooned. Twain turned every mishap—a failed claim, lost bet, or clash with vigilantes—into comic gold. But danger was real. An unflattering article nearly led Twain into a fatal duel; dueling in Nevada was serious, its threat sobering him, refining his satire.

Nature tested Twain, too. The notorious "Washoe Zephyr"—a wild, destructive wind—swept tents away and derailed coaches, serving as his metaphor for frontier chaos. Survival meant constant improvisation—anchoring tents with rocks, jokes with irony. These hardships transformed failure into raw material for creativity. Twain wore his stumbles openly, embracing them as opportunities for humor and self-reinvention.

Steamroller authority was suspect; corrupt officials thrived, and honest people struggled. Justice was often arbitrary, handed out by mobs or corrupt judges. Twain's skepticism of power crystallized here, shaping his literature's enduring suspicion toward those claiming moral certainty.

Twain found inspiration in failed prospectors—men who lost everything yet persisted, often able to joke about disaster. He chronicled their stories, creating mock-heroic tales and rejecting the myth of the flawless protagonist. Twain's self-portraits brimmed with irony—he was always the quick-witted fool, finding laughter even in loss.

Empathy for outsiders became crucial to Twain's writing. He did not just mock failure—he mined it for courage and wisdom. By making himself the butt of jokes—hungry, lost, or scared—he diminished shame and invited readers to recognize their own flaws. His satire wasn't ridicule; it was kinship with everyone who tries, slips, and adapts. In "Roughing It," Twain shows humor as both shelter and glue—a way to summon community from hardship, hope, and transformation. In his vision, the West is a forge, every failure sharpening wit and expanding compassion.

The Jumping Frog Goes Viral—Twain's First National Success

Twain's rise to fame began with a simple mining-camp story. In a rough California bar, he heard an absurd tale of a betting man and his remarkable frog, told with convincing deadpan by the bartender. Twain, always alert for stories echoing the rawness of frontier life, laughed and filed it away. Later, he crafted the tale as "The Celebrated Jumping Frog of Calaveras County" and sent it to The Saturday Press, a struggling New York journal. Its editors were struck by its freshness and sly humor; they published it in 1865. The story went viral, spreading through newspapers nationwide, retold in parlors and saloons, reaching readers weary of moralizing fiction.

"The Jumping Frog" broke new ground with its layered structure. The outside narrator arrives at a mining camp, searching for someone, but is drawn into local Simon Wheeler's digressive, slow-talking tale. Wheeler's recounting of Jim Smiley and his frog builds steadily, growing more absurd with every detail. Twain's brilliance lay in letting Wheeler's voice dominate, creating humor through restraint and repetition. This mirrored actual storytelling—passed by word of mouth, each teller altering the tale. Regional idioms—"ornery," "flopped down," "thrown off"—rooted the story in the West. Twain's attention to repeating phrases—n-grams—made dialogue pop with authenticity.

Reaction was immediate: critics applauded its wit, readers its realism. Twain was soon invited to read his yarns in public, drawing crowds thrilled by his deadpan delivery. His fame leapt—no longer a minor journalist or failed miner, he now belonged nationally. The story's resonance sparked both recognition and new pressures—Twain saw he'd tapped a deep vein of demand for stories rooted in real American life, not sermons.

The "Jumping Frog" marked Twain's new approach—abandoning genteel, moralistic styles of the Eastern literary establishment. Instead, he celebrated ambiguity and comedy in everyday life. His deadpan let readers find their own meaning—he never told them when to laugh. This shifted American storytelling, allowing others to blend regional voices, irony, and local color.

Twain's success changed the literary world. Editors looked beyond East Coast authors; stories from mining camps and riverbeds gained respect as literature, not just amusement. The old barrier between "high" culture and popular tales faded—Americans clamored for fiction drenched in homegrown vernacular.

As Twain's confidence grew, he challenged more literary taboos. Unbound by the demand for refinement, he told stories that mocked authority, lampooned pretension, and reveled in the way American English was actually spoken. One frog—and Twain's knack for pinpointing what made Americans laugh—shifted not just one life but national taste. The chapters ahead trace Twain's evolution, showing how his voice, honed on the river and the frontier, forever changed what it means to be an American writer.

Twain and Technology: A 19th-Century Mind in a 20th-Century World

Mark Twain is remembered as a man rooted in the 19th century, but he was astonishingly modern in his fascination with technology. He adored inventions, gadgets, machines, and scientific breakthroughs. In fact, he held several patents, invested (disastrously) in new machinery, and was one of the first authors to submit a typed manuscript. Twain saw the future coming, and he wanted to be part of it.

This technological enthusiasm shaped his writing in surprising ways. While his stories often depict rustic settings—river towns, steamboats, frontier camps—his essays and speeches reveal a mind captivated by progress. He wrote about telegraphs, typewriters, phonographs, and even early forms of animation. He was an early adopter, not because he wanted prestige but because he believed technology could democratize knowledge and connect people across vast distances.

Twain's humor reflected this, too. He used scientific language as a comedic tool, mixing earnest curiosity with playful skepticism. His satire of pseudoscience in *A Connecticut Yankee in King Arthur's Court* is not merely a joke at the Middle Ages' expense; it is a meditation on the tension between innovation and tradition. Twain understood that technology could elevate society—or expose its follies.

Yet Twain also grasped the human side of progress. His essays reveal concerns about automation, misinformation, and the ways technology could be exploited. These concerns mirror modern conversations about the internet, artificial intelligence, and digital culture. In many ways, Twain predicted the dilemmas of the 21st century.

What makes Twain especially modern is not just his interest
in new devices, but his belief that technology shapes
language. He recognized that the telegraph shortened
sentences, quickened communication, and influenced the
pace of public speech. He understood that each new
invention rewrote the rhythms of conversation.

In celebrating technology while questioning its
consequences, Twain positioned himself at the crossroads
of two centuries. He was both historian and futurist, rooted
in the past yet leaning eagerly toward the modern world—a
duality that helped shape the evolving voice of American
literature.

The Many Masks of Mark Twain: Persona, Performance, and the Public Voice

Mark Twain was not just a writer. He was a performer, a
public figure, and a master of persona. Long before authors
regularly appeared on lecture tours or television interviews,
Twain turned himself into a national character—
recognizable by his white suit, unruly hair, slow drawl, and

How Twain Broke the Rules

Twain routinely violated the "proper" rules taught in 19th-
century English classrooms. And thank goodness he did.

- He ended sentences with prepositions.
- He used contractions—"don't," "ain't," "warn't"
  that were considered vulgar.
- He wrote dialogue exactly as people spoke it, not as
  grammarians wished they would.
- By breaking those rules, Twain helped pull
  American writing out of the parlor and onto the
  porch, where real people lived.

---

mischievous wit. This public identity shaped how Americans heard his words, both on the page and on the stage.

Twain understood instinctively that storytelling was a performance. He developed comedic timing, perfected his pauses, and delivered punchlines with precision. Audiences roared with laughter not only because of what he said, but *how* he said it. This taught the country something important: that language carries music, and that meaning depends as much on rhythm and tone as on vocabulary.

His public persona also influenced the reception of his books. Readers felt they already knew him—a friendly companion with a twinkle in his eye and a joke always within reach. That familiarity created a sense of trust. When Twain criticized society, readers accepted the rebuke because it came from a voice they liked. When he delivered moral truths, they listened because he seemed like an honest man. Twain's persona softened his satire and amplified his authority.

But the persona was also a mask. Behind the humor lay private struggles: debt, grief, self-doubt, and frustration with the nation's direction. Twain sometimes admitted that the public expected him to be funny even when he felt anything but. Yet this tension between the private man and the public performer added complexity to his writing. The humor became deeper, darker, and more layered. The persona shaped the prose, and the prose sustained the persona.

By crafting a public identity, Twain didn't just entertain America—he helped define what it meant to be an American author. He transformed writers from distant figures into cultural personalities. In doing so, he set the stage for the modern literary celebrity and reshaped the relationship between author and audience.

Before he became a novelist, Twain was a journalist—and not a quiet one. He believed newspapers should be lively, humorous, and written in the people's language. His articles attacked dullness the way a terrier attacks rats. In doing so, he helped shift American journalism away from the stiff British model. Reporters after Twain adopted shorter sentences, sharper verbs, and bolder observations. American newspapers became more readable because Twain proved readers preferred energy over elegance.

Why Twain's Writing Still Feels Modern After 150 Years

Readers often remark that Mark Twain "still sounds modern," even though he wrote in the 1800s. This isn't accidental. Twain anticipated many qualities that now define contemporary American writing. First, he embraced the economy of language. While his Victorian contemporaries favored long, ornate sentences, Twain trimmed the excess, crafting prose that was brisk, clear, and conversational. He understood intuitively that readers wanted to feel spoken to, not lectured at.

Second, Twain pioneered the modern narrator: flawed, self-aware, skeptical, and often humorous. Huck Finn's voice in particular feels astonishingly current—casual, observant, emotionally honest. Today's readers gravitate toward narrators who sound like real people, and Twain helped invent that narrative style. His characters do not declaim; they think aloud. They contradict themselves. They blunder into wisdom rather than deliver it.

Third, Twain's themes—race, inequality, greed, corruption, media manipulation—remain strikingly relevant. His satirical approach resembles today's social critics, comedians, and essayists. Twain recognized that humor allowed difficult truths to land without overwhelming the reader. He used comedy as a delivery system for insight, a tactic still employed by writers from Dave Barry to Jon Stewart.

Twain also understood the power of understatement. He rarely hammered a point directly; instead, he nudged readers toward discovery. This subtlety gives his work a timeless quality, letting each generation find new meaning without feeling pushed.

But perhaps the most significant reason Twain feels modern is that he trusted the intelligence of his audience. He didn't explain jokes, didn't tie up every moral thread, and often left ambiguities unresolved. Such confidence in the reader's ability to interpret—something uncommon in his era—is a hallmark of modern writing.

Twain wrote in the 19th century, but his instincts were firmly in the future. His voice set the tone for American literature long before critics had the words to describe what he was doing. That is why he remains not just historic, but contemporary.

People sometimes describe Twain as "simple," as if plain writing required plain thinking. The opposite is true. Twain's simplicity was engineered. It took enormous skill to pare a sentence down to its essential muscle or to build a joke that hit readers across regions and classes. What looked effortless was actually the product of ruthless rewriting. Twain himself said the difference between the right word and the almost-right word was the difference between lightning and the lightning bug. His supposed simplicity became the American ideal—not because it was easy, but because it resonated so clearly with the national character

The Influence of the Tall Tale on American Identity

The American tall tale—outrageous, exaggerated, and delivered with a straight face—was one of Mark Twain's earliest artistic influences. Frontier humor shaped his storytelling long before he became a world-famous author. The tall tale did more than entertain; it helped Americans define themselves as a people who valued wit, resilience, and self-invention.

In the mining camps and river towns where Twain lived as a young man, stories were currency. Men gathered around stoves, bar counters, and campfires to compete in verbal one-upmanship. A good tall tale wasn't just funny; it demonstrated intelligence, creativity, and quick thinking. Twain absorbed this culture deeply. He recognized that humor could reveal truths about character and society more effectively than sober analysis.

The tall tale also matched the national mood. America was expanding westward, confronting the unknown, and inventing its myths in real time. Exaggeration became a way of making sense of vast landscapes, dangerous work, and uncertain futures. The more extreme the story, the more it celebrated the audacity of the frontier spirit.

Twain elevated this tradition. His early success, "The Celebrated Jumping Frog of Calaveras County," took a common frontier structure—a deadpan narrator recounting an absurd local tale—and turned it into literary art. He discovered that exaggeration, when handled with precision, could illuminate human nature. It allowed him to critique vanity, expose gullibility, and reveal both the comedy and tragedy of human aspirations.

But Twain also understood the deeper linguistic value of the tall tale. Its rhythms, pauses, and punchlines formed a distinctly American storytelling cadence. This cadence migrated into his novels, shaping how American characters spoke, argued, joked, and confessed. In many ways, the tall tale was the seed from which much of American humor—and American narrative style—grew.

Today, the tall tale lives on in movies, stand-up comedy, political speeches, and family stories. Its DNA runs through American culture. And Twain, more than anyone else, carried it from the frontier into the realm of literature.

Twain's Global Impact: How the World Heard the American Voice

Mark Twain is often celebrated as an American icon, but his influence extends far beyond national borders. In the late 19th and early 20th centuries, he became one of the most recognizable literary figures in the world—an ambassador of American wit, democracy, and language. Through his books and lecture tours, he introduced international audiences to a distinctly American way of storytelling.

What fascinated foreign readers was not simply Twain's humor but his candor. He spoke plainly, criticized freely, and refused to hide behind politeness. Europeans, accustomed to more formal literary traditions, were electrified by the freshness of his voice. Critics in England noted that Twain wrote with "the honesty of a man who fears no one." Germans admired his precision. Russians appreciated his sympathy for the oppressed. His appeal was universal because he addressed universal themes—freedom, justice, absurdity, human folly—through the lens of everyday speech.

Twain also challenged global assumptions about America. Many Europeans still viewed the United States as culturally immature, lacking refinement or seriousness. Twain turned that perception on its head. His works demonstrated that American literature had its own authority, rooted in lived experience rather than inherited traditions. He made the case, through example rather than argument, that a nation did not need aristocracy to produce art.

His world lectures reinforced this effect. Twain's performances were wildly popular in England, Germany, Australia, India, and South Africa. Audiences saw in him a new type of literary figure: informal, humorous, critical, proud yet self mocking—traits that felt both refreshing and distinctly American.

International authors took notice. Writers such as Rudyard Kipling, Maxim Gorky, and even Joseph Conrad referenced Twain as a model of linguistic innovation. Twain's influence helped open the door for global acceptance of American literature as a serious artistic tradition.

In this way, Twain did more than give America a voice. He helped the world listen to it.

The Hidden Sadness Behind Twain's Humor

Mark Twain's name evokes laughter, but his life was marked by profound sorrow. Behind the jokes and sharp wit lay a man who endured repeated tragedies: the deaths of three of his four children, the early loss of his brother, the bankruptcy that nearly ruined him, and the long illness of his beloved wife, Olivia. These hardships shaped his worldview and infused his writing with an emotional depth often overlooked by readers who focus only on the comedy.

Twain once remarked, "The secret source of humor itself is not joy but sorrow." This was no clever aphorism—it was self-disclosure. Humor became his way of coping, of turning pain into something bearable, even beautiful. Many of his funniest essays were written during moments of crisis. Jokes allowed him to tell the truth indirectly, to express despair without surrendering to it. His humor often carries a bittersweet undertone, a sense that laughter and grief live side by side.

The Twain Effect on Modern American English

Many expressions that feel "naturally American" today gained traction because Twain used them. His influence appears in journalism, comedy, fiction, political speech, and everyday conversation. When Americans choose a short word over a long one, when they value directness, when they distrust pompous phrasing, they are channeling Twain—even if they've never read him. His fingerprints rest on the American tongue.

This emotional complexity enriched his work. In *Huckleberry Finn*, the comedy of Huck and Jim's adventures sits alongside some of the most haunting portrayals of cruelty and injustice in American literature. In *The Mysterious Stranger*, Twain's late-life pessimism surfaces in dark, philosophical reflections on human nature. Even his children's stories—light, imaginative, and gentle—contain shadows if one looks closely enough.

Chapter 3: Twain's Literary Alchemy—Humor, Satire, and the Craft of American Prose

Anatomy of a Tall Tale—Building Suspense and Surprise

Picture an old parlor, its dim lamplight casting shadows as a story begins. Mark Twain dominated these moments—not with bombast, but by steadily forging the unbelievable from the ordinary. With Twain, a tall tale wasn't just a wild exaggeration; it was expertly orchestrated. He started by settling readers into the storyline, piling on oddities until routine scenes spiraled into farce, culminating with a punchline sprung at the precise moment suspense peaked.

In "The Invalid's Story," Twain introduces a narrator tasked with escorting a friend's coffin on a train. The setup is quiet, mundane. A strange odor emerges, growing ever more insistent, fed by worried speculation and the conductor's dire commentary. Suspense tightens—perhaps something's wrong with the corpse. Every paragraph ratchets up discomfort until, at the breaking point, Twain delivers relief: the source isn't decay, but a fetid box of Limburger cheese. The punchline clicks because anticipation and tension have crested, the absurdity sweetened by relief.

"Buck Fanshaw's Funeral" further illustrates Twain's gift. The tale opens with due solemnity, dignified mourners, and sacred ritual. Yet, with every detail—like the preacher fumbling to adapt sermons into mining talk—a sublime unpredictability creeps in. Tributes recount drunken escapades; hymns devolve into discord. Eventually, the preacher, at a loss for spiritual metaphors, defaults to mining jargon. The unfolding absurdity upends expectation and decorum, and laughter erupts as solemnity collapses into chaos.

Much of Twain's magic rests on unreliable narrators and cunning misdirection. In "The Stolen White Elephant," a sober narrator recounts the bizarre disappearance of a gigantic elephant. Bureaucratic, plausible prose enhances the absurdity—every official clue grows increasingly wild. Tone and logic clash, keeping readers uncertain whether to believe, doubt, or laugh. Witness contradictions, absurd theories, and red herrings escalate unpredictability.

Exaggeration is both compass and camouflage. Tiny dilemmas mushroom into disasters—cheese stops a train, etiquette dooms a funeral. Each return to the ordinary is soon shattered by a layer of fresh folly. Disaster looms, then abruptly vanishes, only for events to careen into new realms of nonsense.

Twain's signature move is prolonged solemnity: maintaining straight-faced seriousness until skepticism is overwhelmed. In "The Invalid's Story," the narrator exclaims, "It clung to me like a garment." Each ornate phrase intensifies agitation. In "Buck Fanshaw's Funeral," formal language collides with mining lingo: "He never missed a chance to get drunk or make trouble." This tonal discord amplifies humor, hinting that gravity is always one misstep from slapstick.

Deadpan Delivery—How Understatement Became Twain's Weapon

Twain's comedy thrives on understatement—a poker face layering the outrageous with measured calm. When reading his stories, you sense the narrator lets you in on the joke without a trace of a grin. This deadpan tone is evident in "The Facts Concerning the Recent Carnival of Crime in

Connecticut": a battle of conscience unfolds, yet the unfolding mayhem is logged with sterile precision, as if it were a Sunday routine. Crimes, trials, punishments—the wilder they get, the more neutral the voice. The contrast between absurd events and calm narration intensifies comedy, leaving readers to detect the irony themselves.

Twain's restraint is especially striking when viewed beside Artemus Ward's extravagant, wink-to-the-reader style and Bret Harte's dramatic, ornate prose. Twain stood apart. His dry, unadorned sentences never announce the punchline. Facts are given in ordinary language, trusting audiences to perceive the joke. This subtlety was not just new—it was a revolution in American storytelling, especially in a period dominated by excess emotion and theatricality. Twain's directness, with simple n-grams echoing the vernacular, granted authenticity and immediacy to his humor.

When Twain aimed at societal conventions, his understatement became scalpel-sharp. In "Advice to Youth," his mock-serious suggestions undermine adult authority: obey parents "when it suits you"; avoid lying, "unless necessary." Each pointedly practical tip undercuts the idealism it pretends to teach. Twain doesn't ridicule openly but exposes hypocrisy by letting contradiction reveal itself, achieving quietly devastating comic effect.

Understatement made Twain's political and religious satire even sharper. Instead of ranting about corruption, he describes it blandly as routine, making flaws seem all the more egregious. A legislative fiasco, for Twain, sounds like the only reasonable outcome; preachers' hypocrisy is revealed not through mockery but through exact, emotionless recital. Such indirection protected him from censors while letting the flaws stand unquestioned before the reader.

Religious satire follows suit: rituals are described in detail, the dry tone barely masking a smirk. Twain's emotional neutrality gives readers space to catch the contradictions themselves. These critiques, subtle and familiar, felt more like observations from an insider than distant irrelevance, and thus proved harder to dismiss.

This approach became a blueprint for later humorists. Will Rogers' sly wit ("I don't make jokes; I just watch the government and report the facts") and Dave Barry's deadpan about everyday life echo Twain's tradition: bold truths delivered as if plain facts, humor implicit rather than signposted. Twain's careful use of common words, as described by Zipf's law, lent his writing accessibility and punch, with rare terms providing emphasis just where needed.

For Twain, deadpan wasn't just a style—it was a method for prompting reflection through laughter. He rejected wild stagecraft in favor of subtlety, letting understatement draw readers into the joke instead of dictating it. This quiet self-assurance set a lasting standard for American humor: subtle, sharp, and collaborative with its audience.

Dialect Dialogue—Authenticity, Risks, and Innovations

Twain's deep engagement with the spoken word radically altered American fiction. He listened to the rhythms and quirks of vernacular speech, believing that true American tales needed genuine American voices. From Huck Finn's opening—"You don't know about me without you have read a book by the name of 'The Adventures of Tom Sawyer'; but that ain't no matter"—readers step into the dialects of Missouri, grounded in rough edges he embraced rather than polished away. Contractions, idioms, and colloquialisms made the narrative pulse with authenticity.

This realism, however, drew skepticism. Critics labeled dialect-heavy prose as illegible, even grating. Some argued Twain's dialects reinforced stereotypes, especially among marginalized groups. Today, the debate continues: some view the language in *Huck Finn* as "othering"; some educators fear caricature or inaccessibility. Twain knew these hazards. He intended to depict life as truly spoken, not as polished for literary purity or prescribed by grammar authorities. His dialects vary with each character's history and perspective.

Dialect achieved more than verisimilitude in Twain's hands—it was a means of insight and empathy. Huck's rough speech, formed by hardship yet always flexible and shrewd, contrasts Jim's lyrical, repetition-laden voice. Take Huck's decisive, "All right, then, I'll go to hell"—the phrase's simplicity and honesty cut deeper through dialect than standard English would allow. Jim's proverbs—"I got a hairy breast en dat signifies dat I's gwyne to be rich"—contain humor and hope, shaping character and highlighting social divisions about who "gets" to speak properly.

Twain advanced literary technique by representing speech phonemically, not just via quirky vocabulary but with whole passages echoing natural cadence. In narrative prose, he defaults to standard English—"We went tiptoeing along a path"—but, in dialogue: "We caught fish and talked, and we took a swim to keep off sleepiness." The shift creates a melody, toggling between narrator and character voice.

Dialect carries both humor and gravity. Jim's tales on the raft amuse, but also reveal tenderness; misunderstandings between Huck's literalness and Jim's figurative mind delight, but also humanize. The dialogue's pain surfaces in Jim's longing for his family, the gentle repetitions thick with feeling.

Twain's application of stemming (e.g., "gwyne" for "going") and lemmatization keeps his character voices lean and pulse with life, true to real speech. Even as grammar falters, the steady rhythm ensures clarity and connection.

His commitment ensures fiction that is living, not staged, inviting close listening to what is said—and unsaid. Twain thus redefined American literature's voice, granting stories the sound and dignity of everyday speech.

Societal Skewering—Twain's Satirical Targets in Gilded Age America

Twain trained his satire on Gilded Age vanities—the politics, the fever for quick wealth, and the parade of social strivers. Through works like "The Gilded Age," co-authored with Charles Dudley Warner, Twain lampooned the era's feverish ambition and corruption. Politicians and speculators pursue fortunes with almost comic zeal, while characters like Senator Dilworthy and Colonel Sellers embody the greed and credulity driving both policy and disaster. Politicians switch positions as easily as hats, always aligning with the most lucrative cause. Twain's portrayals mirrored headlines and actual scandals, exaggerating to sharpen the sting.

Twain didn't stop at politics. Speculative bubbles and miracle cures also drew his ire. Newspapers promoted exotic elixirs promising youth and health, which Twain mocked with great relish. He unraveled the hyperbolic language of advertisements, highlighting the absurdity in stories sold to credulous buyers. The same naiveté fueled speculative schemes—from railroads to silver mines—leaving many ruined and a few enriched.

Religion received similar treatment. Revival meetings and sermons are replayed with an ear for contradiction: "Huckleberry Finn" contains a scene where sermons on brotherly love unfold among feuding gunmen. Twain's mock sermons repeat platitudes and contradictions, lampooning ministers who bark against sin yet condone injustice or self-promotion within the church.

Irony is central in works such as "A Connecticut Yankee in King Arthur's Court." Here, a modern engineer's well-intentioned "improvements" unleash chaos in medieval England, ridiculing blind belief in progress and the arrogance of modernity. The resulting spectacle dismantles both nostalgia for tradition and overconfidence in contemporary values.

Twain turned hyperbole into a scalpel, describing reformers "springing up like mushrooms" or conmen who justify swindling the vulnerable as divinely ordained. These exaggerated portraits urged readers to see through such scams.

Most telling was Twain's examination of American optimism—a double-edged ideal. He admired ingenuity, but saw hope transform into delusion. In essays on expansion and destiny, Twain ridiculed the conviction that America's way should be everyone's, exposing the dangers of unchecked ambition.

Twain's targets echo into modern times—scandals fueled by lobbyists, miraculous new diets or investments, and viral get-rich-quick fads. His techniques—parody, irony, and exaggeration—stay relevant for exposing how progress often masks folly and optimism feeds self-deception.

Politicians still promise reforms before sinking into scandals. Media personalities market miracle goods. Financial frenzies grip the public. Twain's wit would instantly recognize and lampoon these familiar scripts; the cycles endure.

Annotated Masterclass—Dissecting Humor in "Huckleberry Finn" and "Tom Sawyer"

Twain's mastery shines brightest in scenes rich with comic detail. Recall Tom Sawyer's fence-painting: what starts as dreaded punishment morphs into coveted privilege. Tom feigns joy—"Does a boy get a chance to whitewash a fence every day?"—prompting friends to bribe their way into his work. Phrases repeat—"does a boy get a chance," "whitewash a fence"—to underline the ludicrous value shift. Fast dialogue and concise sentences compress the comedy. The real punch is in reversal: authority turns on its head, and work becomes reward, a sly jab at how value and power are constructed and perceived.

Tom's ruse operates on many levels. Children enjoy the mischief; adults perceive how people crave exclusivity and are manipulated by appearances. Work and status are ridiculed, with Twain's wit illuminating the systemic absurdity beneath.

Switch to "Huckleberry Finn," where Huck and Jim's raft banter brims with wit and philosophical depth. Jim's insistence—"Why doan' he talk like a man?"—and Huck's logical but unconvincing replies journey in comical circles, with Jim persistently returning to first principles.

Twain embeds jokes for all: children enjoy the playful back-and-forth, while adults see deeper commentaries on language, perception, and social difference. The quick rhythm and misdirection—Huck assumes he'll outwit Jim, but Jim prevails—keep the exchange lively.

Irony suffuses these conversations, such as when Huck ponders, "What's the use you learning to do right, when…it ain't no trouble to do wrong, and the wages is just the same?" Twain's irony deconstructs morality's contradictions, exposing empty lessons and probing what we call "right."

Reversal resurfaces when Tom devises elaborate escape plans in "Huckleberry Finn." Tom's insistence on drama—digging with spoons, sending blood-stained notes—emphasizes the farce behind heroics. Twain's language amplifies the madness, satirizing overcomplicated action.

Twain's comic range runs from slapstick to biting wit. Each laugh doubles as commentary or character insight. Every comic turn is precisely timed, every reversal or irony hiding a barbed point about power, freedom, or belonging.

Twain's greatest comedic achievement is purposeful laughter—every prank or joke lays bare the absurdities of social norms and human conduct. Comedy becomes a tool for truth, never mere entertainment.

Twain's Writing Toolkit—Notebooks, Marginalia, and Creative Process

Twain's genius owed much to diligent notekeeping and revision, not just raw insight. His surviving notebooks offer a glimpse at the restless interplay of observation and experimentation behind the humor. Twain jotted down fragments everywhere—in trains, hotels, sleepless nights—with overheard phrases, character sketches, or stray puzzles about human nature. Some scrawls barely form sentences: "Saw man in barbershop—face like a boiled potato—use for villain?" Others stretch into expanded storylines or the rhythm of a regional saying. Twain gathered news clippings, snatches of conversation, and stray anecdotes. Inspiration was actively pursued, not passively awaited.

Revision was essential, not optional. Twain pored over drafts, adjusting structure, reworking punchlines, or shifting perspective until his instincts matched the page's tone and timing. Marginalia in manuscripts for "A Connecticut

Yankee in King Arthur's Court" expose this process: lines are scratched out ("too slow"), paragraphs shuffled, and jokes re-timed. Humor was built, tested, and refined—sometimes tossed aside if it disrupted pace or focus. Scenes went through multiple versions in his notebooks as he tirelessly honed delivery and impact.

Real-life events furnished Twain's literary gold. Eavesdropping for unique expressions or unexpected reactions, he scribbled down ideas for possible transformation. Letters to friends document his willingness to admit when a story or joke misfired, turning failures into learning tools. Twain was quick to discard anecdotes that didn't work, or rework plotlines that didn't deliver.

Performance shaped much of Twain's comedy before publishing. Public readings and lectures functioned as live testing grounds—Twain watched for audience reaction, adjusted timing for suspense, and rewrote on the fly if necessary. Not every joke survived, but those that provoked laughter were marked for future use. Audience feedback informed every change, with Twain noting which lines caused "uproarious laughter."

Twain's creative process was both disciplined and playful—relentlessly field-testing words in living rooms and on stage, fine-tuning phrases for maximum punch. "Try this line with German accent"; "Shorten this bit—too wordy"; such notations reveal a scientist tinkering with hypotheses, each variation judged for its unique effect. Some stories never left the notebook; others evolved through years of retooling before achieving finished form.

Chapter 4: Gilded Age Chronicler—Twain in Context: Politics, Progress, and Prejudice

The Gilded Age Unmasked—Twain's Critique of Corruption and Excess

Imagine the extravagant lobby of a Washington hotel in 1873—lamplight flickering, cigar smoke curling, and men in fine clothes exchanging clandestine deals. Money slides across tables with a nod; ambition overshadows principle. This is the tableau Mark Twain dissected in "The Gilded Age: A Tale of Today," where superficial progress barely conceals a surge of greed, speculation, and manipulation. Twain not only observed this spectacle but meticulously exposed it in his fiction.

Collaborating with Charles Dudley Warner, Twain created "The Gilded Age," both a satirical novel and a probing diagnosis of postwar America. Its title became synonymous with an era radiantly gilded on the surface yet rotten beneath. Twain lampooned the feverish gold-rush mentality gripping society. Through the Hawkins family's frantic pursuit of quick riches, he distilled the tragic experience of Americans seduced by land speculation or the allure of effortless government fortune. Lobbyists swarm Congress, votes go to the highest bidder, and speculators rig land values through rumor and fraud. Twain's sharpest satire targets politicians who turn public office into a private stage, seeking enrichment under the pretense of service.

Twain used irony and hyperbole to full effect. His characters' ambitions expand to ridiculous heights. Senators are parodies of their own importance; their grand speeches barely veil their self-interest. Land agents conjure entire towns out of marshes, preying on hopeful farmers who struggle even to read the contracts. Twain's humor is consistent and biting; everyone is a target, including those with earnest intentions. In episode after episode, hope stumbles into farce, and trust morphs into betrayal.

The Hawkins family's endless scheming forms the novel's moral center. Colonel Sellers, eternally optimistic and sure his next gamble is infallible, personifies America's speculative mania. Every new project—land grants, phantom railroads—falters, but Sellers perseveres, convinced fortune waits just ahead. Twain's tone is analytical, not vindictive; he shows how hope can blind honest souls, fostering self-deception.

Twain was intimately familiar with this cycle. He himself chased big ideas, swinging between prosperity from writing and near-bankruptcy from risky ventures. His letters reveal mounting skepticism toward "robber barons" and industrial tycoons who disguised greed as national mission (see APA list: 15). Twain criticized these magnates privately for their lax ethics and for exploiting patriotic rhetoric to rationalize avarice.

His satire was grounded in reality: the era's real scandals often surpassed fiction. The infamous Credit Mobilier scheme siphoned millions from federal coffers into the pockets of railroad tycoons and politicians; public outrage faded, and politicians returned to power unscathed. Twain also lampooned Boss Tweed, who transformed Tammany Hall into a profit machine while posing as a man of the people. The gold market crash, engineered by Jay Gould and James Fisk, revealed how a few speculators could upend the entire economy through mere rumor.

Twain constructed his fictional world from newspaper headlines and public scandals, alchemizing current events into timeless literature. The mockery of land grant mania mirrored the real obsession with western expansion, where bribery or fraud redrew maps overnight. This blend of satire and reportage blurs the lines of fiction and reality—Twain wanted readers to see beyond appearances, question promises, and ask who truly prospers from supposed innovation.

His critique remains relevant. Exaggerated characters and comic disasters bring to light dilemmas that endure: unchecked ambition, progress marred by exploitation, and hope morphing into vanity. Rather than simply amuse, Twain presses readers to consider how easily societies slip from advancement to predation.

Race, Class, and Contradiction—Twain's Social Commentary and Its Limits

Mark Twain's portrayals of race and class reveal both his bold critiques and the limits of his era. In "Adventures of Huckleberry Finn," Jim emerges as a vital, complex figure—a Black man defying the stereotypes of his day. Twain grants Jim wit, feeling, and loyalty; Jim's friendship with Huck exposes the hypocrisy of a "civilized" society that condones cruelty. Yet, even as Twain undercuts racist conventions, he sometimes reinforces them—using period dialect, comic relief, or superstition to provoke laughter. His frequent use of racial slurs, though intended to reflect historical reality, continues to incite discomfort and prompts debate about whether satire mitigates or amplifies harm.

Twain's concern for social justice grew as he aged. By the late 19th century, he publicly opposed American imperialism, aligning with the Anti-Imperialist League and condemning U.S. policies in the Philippines and Puerto Rico as betrayals of founding ideals. He denounced figures such as Belgium's King Leopold for colonial atrocities, calling imperialism straightforward theft masked as progress. Twain defended Chinese immigrants against the Chinese Exclusion Act, rebuffing nativism and championing equal rights. He maintained that democracy was hollow if it excluded citizens based on race. Lynchings and legal failures to protect Black rights further sharpened his advocacy.

However, contradictions linger in Twain's satire. Modern critics examine whether, by repeatedly invoking stereotypes, Twain genuinely humanizes his subjects or inadvertently bolsters prejudices. "Huckleberry Finn's" repetition of slurs spotlights social brutality, but its effect remains troubling ("Controversy at Cherry Hill - Huck Finn Teachers Guide" APA list: 6). "The Adventures of Tom Sawyer" introduces "Injun Joe"—a threatening outsider shaped more by racist tropes than individual depth. Twain hints at Joe's pain and isolation, but these nuances sit uneasily alongside the demands to serve as a villain, reflecting the period's anxieties about Native Americans. Such tensions show how even insurgent writers can sustain the patterns they hope to expose.

Class is another thread throughout Twain's work, seen in dreamers, hustlers, and strugglers. In "The Gilded Age," ordinary people are seduced by schemes that promise quick wealth and deliver disappointment. Twain's characters are rarely born villains; they are products of systemic economic strains and the myth that success is always attainable. Their failures are a mix of humor and tragedy, exposing how visions of upward mobility are ripe for manipulation. Twain's short stories center on working-class figures— miners, printers, and riverboat hands—whose hardships spotlight the gulf between American promise and everyday reality. Twain's empathy for these characters arises from his own experiences with poverty and the uncertainty of frontier life; his central characters are often skeptical, wry, and observant.

Twain's scorn for privilege underlies much of his satire. He ridicules the powerful yet exposes how the poor are set against one another in the mad scramble for dignity and survival. His antagonists are often petty officials as well as major tycoons, but the stories reveal how ambition and desperation can seduce anyone into complicity.

Twain's treatment of race and class is thus complex and contested—direct in its criticism but marred by historical limits. Readers debate whether he challenged prejudice enough or simply repeated the stereotypes of his time. Nevertheless, Twain forced audiences to confront uncomfortable truths: the toll of freedom, the endurance of bigotry, and the dreams dashed when schemes collapse. Rather than send readers away with pat answers, his fiction generates urgent questions, sparking vigorous reflection even now.

The Civil War's Shadow—Shaping Twain's Views on Humanity and Conflict

The Civil War left a deep mark on American letters, and for Mark Twain, it left both personal and collective scars. Twain's own involvement was brief: in 1861, he joined the Marion Rangers, a ragtag Confederate militia. Their resolve fizzled quickly. Twain later, with irony, described his "retirement" at the faintest threat—puncturing fantasy with reality.

He did not romanticize his military stint. In "The Private History of a Campaign That Failed," Twain reimagines his youthful folly as a tale of young men playing soldier until they cause a stranger's death by mistake. That act shatters their bravado, replacing excitement with remorse—

rerouting the narrative from glory to moral reckoning. Through these stories, Twain doubted the very idea of heroism, pressing readers to recognize the uncertainty and ambiguity beneath the martial mythos. War, for Twain, was stripped of gallant gloss and revealed as a stage for confusion, mistakes, and pain.

Conversations with actual veterans deepened Twain's skepticism. The stories they told—of chaos, horror, and disappointment—transformed his view. Twain saw soldiers returning, broken and disillusioned, and increasingly doubted mass morality. He became wary of groupthink and skeptical of political rhetoric invoking honor to justify violence. Twain realized war was seldom waged for causes as noble as those invoked.

Twain also documented the struggle for national healing. He acknowledged nostalgia's potency but refused to gloss over suffering. In satirical essays, he rejected "Lost Cause" sentimentality and the romanticization of defeat. Twain ridiculed orations that recast the Confederacy as noble, refusing to let rhetoric rewrite the realities of slavery, loss, and division.

His postwar letters reveal tensions over memories and reconciliation. Twain described uneasy ceremonies reuniting enemies while old animosities lingered. Correspondence bristles with his frustration at the slow pace of true healing, as grudges persisted despite public gestures. The railroad may have reconnected North and South, but emotional distance remained.

His writing before and after the war tracks a personal evolution: early nostalgia for Missouri's river-town freedom shifts to postwar realism—landscapes scarred, towns changed, and people shaped by grief and cynicism. Twain's journey mirrored a nation's move from innocence toward recognition shaped by ordeal.

Twain always confronted hard truths, refusing to prettify the past. His blend of satire, memoir, and fiction documents both wounds suffered and lessons learned—a record of violence's lasting mark on people, memory, and conscience. Twain's nuanced perspective encourages readers to remember not only what was lost, but what was illuminated: fear mingled with courage, pride with shame, and a complicated legacy of conflict and healing.

Gender and the New Woman—Twain's Complex Portrayals and Private Beliefs

When reading Twain, women quickly stand out—sometimes as muses, sometimes as agents of change or rebels—always reflecting the tensions of their time. Becky Thatcher in "The Adventures of Tom Sawyer" exemplifies these complexities. She's the object of Tom's fascination, but not a passive figure; Becky's stubbornness, pride, and resourcefulness, especially in the cave scene, move the story forward. She's more than a damsel or prize; she reveals the assumptions and anxieties of her age, embodying both innocence and the ambiguous power ascribed to women.

As Twain's perspective evolved, his satire extended to the changing world of women. He lampooned the earnestness of women's clubs and reform movements, poking fun at their debates and politics. Behind the humor, however, was a grudging respect for these women's tenacity and intelligence. Twain observed that, even if sincere or occasionally absurd, their activism introduced new energies into public life. His critique is rarely scathing; it often shows discomfort with evolving roles rather than outright opposition.

Strong women in Twain's life shaped his developing opinions. His wife, Olivia Langdon Clemens (Livy)—his closest critic and confidante—helped refine his work, offering crucial edits and posing moral questions. Their correspondence shows genuine intellectual collaboration and growing respect. His daughter Susy, inquisitive and self-possessed, inspired pride and worry as she stepped outside the norms set for young women. Twain's heartfelt letters to Susy demonstrate his admiration, as well as trepidation about the shifting world she would inhabit.

With national debates over women's education and suffrage intensifying, Twain became more outspoken. He increasingly advocated for women's voting rights and education, insisting that denying them equality was incompatible with American ideals. As his thinking shifted, so too did his fiction. In "A Connecticut Yankee in King Arthur's Court," Twain introduced assertive female characters—women determined to learn, lead, and even organize collective action during crisis. Here, the emerging "New Woman" of the 1890s is not a side note but a dynamic presence in the narrative.

Twain as America's First Literary Celebrity

When Twain toured the country giving lectures, he wasn't just entertaining crowds—he was teaching America how America sounded. The jokes, pauses, dialects, and phrasing he used on stage became national expressions. Thousands of Americans adopted his turns of phrase without realizing it. His public persona reinforced his literary one: he became the ambassador of a new American voice, not through essays or manifestos, but through laughter. When a nation laughs together, it learns to speak together.

Nevertheless, contradiction shadows Twain's gender politics. In personal essays, he supported suffrage but sometimes relied on comic stereotypes—nagging wives, confused husbands, the "battle of the sexes." Pieces like "On the Decay of the Art of Lying" and "Advice to Girls" lampoon marriage and domestic intrigue, mixing skepticism with sympathy for women hemmed in by convention. Marital life is presented as affectionate but absurd; equality is desired but rarely fully realized.

Twain's commentary on divorce is revealing. He never divorced Livy, but he wrote candidly about the misery of couples trapped by law or custom. He maintained that companionship mattered more than tradition or religious dictate—a progressive view for his era, though still circumscribed by inherited gender models. In his letters and essays, Twain wavered between calls for reform and remnants of stereotype.

His female characters resist reductive summaries. Some—like the inventive Sandy in "A Connecticut Yankee" or the formidable Aunt Polly—show autonomy that rivals any male counterpart. Others remain stuck in nostalgia's web, depicted more as objects of desire or ridicule than agents of change. Twain's literature reflects an era of transformation—extending hope for progress while simultaneously expressing unease about what change means.

Twain chronicled America's gender evolution as both participant and observer. He met new possibilities for women with a blend of admiration and uncertainty, offering portrayals that are vibrant yet rarely simplistic. Through his struggle, we see literature's power to both mirror and accelerate social metamorphosis.

Twain and the Machine—Technology, Inventions, and Modernity

Among his contemporaries, Twain most eagerly embraced the spirit of invention—with both fascination and risk. His interest in technology was genuine, shaped by equal parts excitement and apprehension. Twain involved himself personally in the era's innovations, sometimes to his detriment. His backing of the Paige typesetter—a sophisticated, but overly complex, typesetting machine— was his greatest folly. He invested heavily, hoping it would transform publishing and secure his fortune. But night after night spent watching its construction led only to disappointment; the machine, always near perfection, perpetually broke down. The failure exhausted Twain financially and emotionally and served as a cautionary tale about trusting in technology.

These experiences informed Twain's writings. Railroads, telegraphs, and steamboats are not just backdrops in his stories but drivers of change and disruption. "Life on the Mississippi" blends nostalgia for steamboats with a sense of impending loss. The telegraph—novel and miraculous— symbolizes both faster communication and new confusion. Railroads change the landscape, promising progress while undermining old ways. Twain never lets technology remain simply ornamental; he weaves it into metaphors about onward rush and the price of modernity.

"A Connecticut Yankee in King Arthur's Court" is Twain's brightest reflection on technology's two-edged nature. An American engineer transported to medieval England brings knowledge of gunpowder, steam engines, and the telegraph. His innovations dazzle but also destabilize, as every technological leap spreads not only promise but envy and unease. Twain's lesson is that technological progress may disrupt without fully healing or improving society.

Twain's real-life engagement with inventors enriched this outlook. He befriended Nikola Tesla, whose pioneering work in electricity amazed him. Twain visited Tesla's lab in New York, posed for photographs, and relished the spectacle of wireless energy and glowing lights. Their relationship shows mutual respect: Tesla for Twain's wit, Twain for Tesla's scientific imagination. At world's fairs and expositions, Twain rubbed shoulders with entrepreneurs showcasing the latest marvels—experiences that inspired his fiction but also deepened his skepticism. Each breakthrough was shadowed by a host of forgotten failures.

Twain never blindly celebrated progress. He reveled in poking fun at modern gadgets—alarm clocks that malfunctioned, stoves that exploded, early automobiles that confounded their drivers, telephones that interrupted more than clarified. His stories often recount failed inventions, satirizing both aspiration and folly at the root of technological change.

In later writings, he acknowledged his mistakes—financial losses, wasted efforts—but cast them with irony. He understood that machines could deliver freedom or foster new dependency. The telegraph spread information and misinformation; the railroad opened frontiers but erased communities. Twain was not anti-technology, but he distrusted any claim of easy progress.

Twain's enduring question: Do new machines improve us or simply distract? He saw American society hurrying forward, rarely pausing to ask where it was headed or what would be lost. His stories invite readers to marvel, but also to question; each new tool exacts a cost, hope is endlessly tied to risk, and every leap forward subtly reshapes society and self. Twain's fascination with invention becomes a call to approach change critically, balancing skepticism with curiosity.

Annotated Maps and Timelines—Visualizing Twain's America

To grasp Twain's reach and the forces shaping his era, visualizing his experiences against the kinetic background of 19th-century America is enlightening. Picture Twain's movements: from Hannibal's quiet riverbanks, to Nevada's mining towns, to New York's bustling streets, then further still to London and Vienna. Twain's lecture tours were more than financial necessity; each brought him new perspectives and fresh material. Charting these journeys mirrors the nation's dynamism—western migration, rapid urbanization, and a mesh of railroads and telegraph lines crisscrossing the landscape. Comparing his real travels along the Mississippi with his fictional characters' odysseys, especially Huck and Jim's, reveals the river's physical and metaphorical role: a conduit from childhood through national mythology to social critique.

A timeline integrating Twain's literary milestones and American historical events offers insight into their dialogue. Setting the publication of "Tom Sawyer" alongside railroad expansion or the appearance of "Huckleberry Finn" with the emergence of Jim Crow laws triggers new realizations. As "A Connecticut Yankee in King Arthur's Court" arrives during the era of the Chicago World's Fair, America is simultaneously celebrating invention and confronting unrest. Lining up Twain's books with technological breakthroughs like the telephone or electric light showcases his responsiveness to constant upheaval, revealing how fiction and fact coexist in his work.

Charts on Hannibal's population growth illuminate Twain's nostalgia for small-town life. Early census data depict a tranquil river community mushrooming with the arrival of steamboats and commerce. These visuals anchor the unease and nostalgia permeating Twain's stories—the sense that transformation brought both excitement and anxiety. Look at similar graphs for western boomtowns: spikes and declines in population as gold prospects rose and fell or rail routes redrew destinies. These patterns taught Twain the volatility of prosperity and the swift collapse of dreams.

"Twain's War on Pretentious Language"

Mark Twain had a lifelong grudge against inflated, pretentious writing. To him, any writer who hid behind long Latin words was likely hiding weak ideas as well. Twain believed that the clearest sentence was usually the truest one, and he spent his career trimming the fat from American prose. When he mocked politicians, clergy, or newspaper editors, he often did it by repeating their words exactly as they had spoken them—bloated, pompous, frequently ridiculous. The reader didn't need Twain to add satire; **the satire was already in their vocabulary**. By elevating plain speech and exposing hollow speech, Twain reset the American standard: clarity first, honesty second, elegance third.

Graphics tracing immigration, race legislation, and industrial expansion shed light on deeper social conflicts underlying Twain's narratives. A bar graph charting anti-Chinese laws highlights Twain's outspoken defense of immigrants, while graphs juxtaposing factory growth and labor unrest clarify why his characters often manifest restlessness and skepticism for progress. These visuals expose the forces of change shaping Twain's world just as starkly as his prose does.

Story maps can track meaning and movement alike. "Huckleberry Finn's" journey is both concrete and symbolic. Annotated maps pinpoint key sites—St. Petersburg, Jackson's Island, each town marking a crisis. Notations reveal when narrative moments arise from real history—steamboat accidents, racial violence, feuds—all grounding the adventure in reality.

Pairing Twain's personal milestones with national events reveals convergence: his financial ruin coincides with the Panic of 1893, affecting millions. European tours reflect America's rising ambitions and anxieties about its world role. Such visual correlations clarify why Twain's later works grow darker as faith in reform dims.

Ultimately, these visualizations do more than inform; they create resonance—a sense that Twain's era, like our own, was alive with flux and uncertainty. Maps show movement as destiny; timelines couple personal and public drama; statistical charts lay bare the social undercurrents animating his fiction. Overlaying Twain's narratives with these analytics reveals how he tamed chaos into story and transformed unpredictability into wit and reflection.

In summary, to understand America through Twain is to reject easy boundaries and static definitions. His world was constantly moving—marked by migration, innovation, conflict, and dreams that outgrew their maps. In the next chapter, we'll examine how Twain navigated the labyrinth of fame and truth, fame's pleasures and snares, and his evolving quest for creative honesty.

Congratulations! You've made it this far!

I hope you're enjoying *Mark Twain And The Making of American Literature*, and that you continue reading the rest of it…

Many potential readers consider the quality and quantity of reviews a book has earned, and the better the reviews, the more a seller prioritizes it.

All you have to do is locate this book online, scroll down to where it says "Write a customer review," and follow the directions to write a much-appreciated review. It doesn't have to be long. They recommend at least a few sentences.

Thanks much in advance.

Please keep reading,

Blake Whitworth

Chapter 5: Masterworks and Margins—A Deep Dive Into Twain's Major and Overlooked Works

The Adventures of Tom Sawyer—Boyhood, Freedom, and the Illusion of Innocence

Imagine a sunburned boy perched atop a split-rail fence, eyes bright with mischief as he surveys the sleepy Mississippi streets. This iconic image epitomizes the myth Mark Twain masterfully weaves in *The Adventures of Tom Sawyer*. But reading Tom's escapades reveals that Twain provides more than nostalgia for lost youth; he probes the tensions of American ideals about freedom and innocence.

Twain rejects the notion of childhood as a refuge from adulthood, instead depicting it as a competitive proving ground. Nowhere is this clearer than in the fence-whitewashing episode. What starts as labor—Tom's punishment for mischief—quickly becomes a means of status. By cleverly turning the chore into a coveted privilege and demanding payment in trinkets or apples for each brushstroke, Tom turns peers into willing participants. Twain thus encapsulates social maneuvering and group psychology into a single afternoon, exposing how innocence swiftly shifts to guile. The scene distills small-town society: status is fluid, persuasion outweighs rules, and adult authority is constantly subverted.

Jackson's Island, where Tom, Huck, and Joe flee to play at piracy, pushes fantasy to its limits. Their adventure isn't mere escapism—it's a trial of rebellion and self-rule. Yet the boys' freedom is incomplete: guilt and homesickness set in, and a storm nearly overwhelms them. Twain's irony is stark—the attempt to escape authority yields hard lessons in responsibility and the dangers lurking even within imaginative play.

St. Petersburg is lovingly, yet skeptically, painted—bursting with rituals: tedious sermons, classroom recitations, Sunday School's quest for Bible tickets. Twain lampoons these customs, exposing performative piety and showy religiosity. Meanwhile, children adopt their own codes—secret handshakes, blood oaths, elaborate games—mirroring and parodying adults. Superstition and folklore permeate decisions: dead cats banish warts, howling dogs portend doom, and midnight graveyard visits signify coming of age. For Tom and his friends, these beliefs structure their world, offering strategies for interpreting danger in a society where adult authority is inconsistent.

Humor, suspense, and irony power Twain's scenes. In the graveyard, as Tom and Huck hunt for a magical cure, they stumble onto Injun Joe's murder. Twain crafts tension with hushed dialogue, sensory cues—gravel crunching, lanterns flickering—before the sudden burst of violence severs innocence. Fear and secrecy pull the boys from childhood directly into moral quandaries. Later, Becky Thatcher's ordeal in McDougal's Cave escalates tension; lost in darkness, she and Tom teeter on the brink of starvation and despair, saved by Tom's cleverness. Ironically, Tom's reputation for trickery becomes their salvation, albeit dangerously.

Tom Sawyer endures precisely because it straddles myth and realism. Early illustrations play up Tom's bravado; later films often soften or romanticize him. Scholars debate: Is Tom a self-serving antihero or a resourceful survivor? Some argue Twain caricatures Americana; others see a precise, affectionate critique (The Adventures of Tom

Sawyer Study Guide - Mark Twain). This tension ensures the novel remains relevant, reinterpreted by each new generation.

Ultimately, *Tom Sawyer* is central to American childhood myth because it acknowledges pain beneath bravado, the cost of freedom, and innocence's fragility. Twain's blend of humor and suspense draws readers to a world where each scraped knee and whispered secret is part of a deeper journey of growing up.

Adventures of Huckleberry Finn—Race, Rebellion, and the American Conscience

Opening *Adventures of Huckleberry Finn*, we encounter a world ridden with prejudice, contradiction, and opportunity. Huck's journey down the river is more than escape; it's a test of values. The river is a sanctuary and battleground, as law, conscience, and society clash. On the shore, Huck confronts adults intent on "sivilizing" him, legal systems blind to cruelty, and communities upholding slavery. Yet aboard the raft, a separate world forms. Here, Huck's alliance with Jim, an enslaved man seeking freedom, becomes central.

Twain the Satirist vs. Twain the Linguist

Readers often think Twain's mission was humor. In truth, his mission was **truth**—and humor was his scalpel. His satire exposed dishonesty, hypocrisy, cruelty, and self-deception. But his language—sharp, flexible, mischievous—made those truths unforgettable. His influence on American speech is inseparable from his influence on American conscience.

Huck's growth is revealed through his changing relationship with Jim. Twain builds their friendship with nuance, interweaving humor, suspense, and revelations. Jim's dignity shows in his devotion to family and patient endurance of Huck's jokes. A pivotal scene—the "fog" episode—finds Huck fooling Jim, denying their separation during a fog. Jim's pain is plain: "En all you wuz thinkin' 'bout wuz how you could make a fool uv ole Jim wid a lie." Huck's remorse changes everything: "It made me feel so mean I could almost kiss his foot to get him to take it back." For Huck, Jim becomes fully human—subverting ingrained prejudice and catalyzing growth.

Where Huck's moral crisis peaks is deciding whether to betray Jim. Huck ponders writing to Ms. Watson, Jim's owner, convinced he'd "go to hell" for helping an enslaved man escape. Nuanced and understated, Huck chooses, "All right, then, I'll go to hell." The scene isn't melodramatic—it's a lone act of rebellion against corrupted morality. Huck's private decision challenges readers to question when custom should yield to conscience.

Debate continues over Twain's use of dialect and racial language. Jim's vernacular has been criticized for caricature, but many see authentic agency and depth. Classroom controversies persist: some ban the novel for slurs, others contend that facing its language is key to confronting America's history (Cherry Hill Controversy, Huck Finn Teachers Guide). Advocates highlight Jim's perceptiveness—his understanding of omens, his exposure of white hypocrisy—while detractors note episodes where Jim is the target of pranks or made comic.

Huckleberry Finn's influence is immense. Hemingway declared, "All modern American literature comes from one book by Mark Twain called Huckleberry Finn." Twain's direct style, taboo topics, and focus on marginalized figures altered fiction's course. Literary heirs—Ellison, Morrison, Wallace—engage with Twain, critiquing his blind spots while building on his breakthrough use of voice and perspective.

Twain's satirical legacy persists. Writers like Vonnegut and Colson Whitehead adopt his method: wielding dialect and irony to expose hypocrisy, blending humor with critique. Twain's "show, don't tell" approach—letting character and conversation carry meaning—remains vital. The Mississippi endures as a symbol—erasing old codes, testing new truths.

Huckleberry Finn is both a protest and a quest. Huck's transformation grows from shared danger and experience with Jim. Their journey, like moral progress, is uncertain and unresolved. Readers return to this novel because it refuses easy answers, continually pressing us to reckon with our conscience. The language stings, the questions persist, and the challenge endures.

A Connecticut Yankee—Satire, Science, and the Perils of Progress

A Connecticut Yankee in King Arthur's Court is among Twain's most daring works—part parody, part prophetic vision, and completely unsparing about human folly. The comic premise is striking: Connecticut engineer Hank Morgan is knocked unconscious and wakes in medieval England. Yet, beneath this whimsical surface, Twain sets up a clash of eras and worldviews that satirizes both medieval fantasy and modern hubris. Morgan's faith in science and progress becomes a destabilizing force.

Morgan's inventions in Camelot—most famously the electric fence—serve as both practical jokes and biting metaphors. He introduces telegraphs, factories, and public schools, hoping to remake Camelot in modern America's image, arming peasants with knowledge and tools. The farcical image of armor-clad knights shocked by electricity is funny, but Twain's point cuts deeper: both medieval credulity and industrial arrogance are dangerous. Not all progress is improvement; every "advance" unbalances the social order.

Hank Morgan isn't content to observe; he's a reformer convinced rationality can fix any problem. By outwitting Merlin, predicting a solar eclipse, and rising to authority as "The Boss," he exerts technological and political dominance. Yet every advance breeds resistance and confusion, alienating those he leads. The dialogue reveals Morgan's blindness: claiming he will "civilize" old England, he overlooks deepening violence. Twain's irony is sharp—ambitious reforms breed revolt and fear as often as hope.

The novel's climax is devastating. Morgan's technological marvels culminate in mechanized slaughter: he wires the battlefield with explosives and electric fences. Knights perish by machine, their courage irrelevant against impersonal force. Twain's vivid scene foresees the coming age of industrialized warfare—a warning about the dangers of unchecked technology.

Twain's skepticism mirrored personal disappointment. Failed ventures like the Paige typesetter cost him dearly (A Connecticut Yankee in King Arthur's Court). The novel channels this bitterness into a warning: progress isn't always enlightenment; reason alone can lead to destruction. Technological solutions may breed chaos if untempered by humility and ethical reflection.

A Connecticut Yankee is seen as both science fiction and dystopian satire, influencing Orwell and Vonnegut, who ask if technology liberates or ensnares. Debate continues: is Morgan a visionary or a cautionary figure? Twain refuses to clarify, retaining ambiguity. His humor masks deeper unease about tradition and innovation. The novel asks if inventions serve humanity, or if, ultimately, we become their instruments.

Pudd'nhead Wilson and the Tragedy of Identity

In *Pudd'nhead Wilson*, Twain deconstructs the notion of fixed identity, revealing how law, birth, and coincidence shape fate. The heart of the story is Roxy, a light-skinned enslaved woman, swapping her one-sixteenth Black baby for her master's white son. The children's fates are swapped: Tom lives with privilege, the true heir endures slavery. Twain highlights how arbitrary race, law, and convention define destiny, employing the "switched at birth" device to dissect racism's cruelty and illogic.

Fingerprints, a motif Twain explores with fascination for forensic science, feature heavily. Pudd'nhead Wilson, the town's nominal fool, is dismissed for his eccentric interest in fingerprints and aphorisms ("Few things are harder to put up with than the annoyance of a good example."), But it is ultimately vindicated. His fingerprint collection unravels the truth, and scientific inquiry defeats social prejudice, giving the novel a progressive edge.

Roxy's story resonates deeply—her love for her child cannot protect him from racism's "one drop" rule, classifying anyone with Black ancestry as Black and thus enslaved. Watching Tom grow into a selfish and cruel adult is devastating. Twain lends Roxy empathy and irony: her desperate act leads to personal tragedy and the broader exposure of society's arbitrary cruelty.

Twain's courtroom satire exposes how justice is warped by bias. The trial pits heritage and "good breeding" against evidence, while townsfolk ignore glaring truths. It's only science—fingerprints—that exposes falsehoods. Twain strips the courthouse of dignity, presenting law as performance and prejudice, not impartiality.

Politics in Dawson's Landing is equally farcical: elections are driven by rumor and self-interest, and leaders are more concerned with appearances than sincerity. The town moves in ritual, sustaining myth and hierarchy by fear or habit.

Irony dominates this novel. Readers observe the true identities long before characters, layering tension and inevitability as Tom's schemes unravel. Wilson's witty aphorisms sting when weighed against the unfolding disaster. There's scant redemption—Tom faces exposure, Roxy endures further loss—with individual anguish mirroring systemic injustice.

The story's humor is far darker than Twain's previous works. Each reversal feels brutal: thieves raised as gentlemen, a mother's sacrifice backfiring, science revealing only brokenness. Twain resists easy comfort, allowing bleakness to underscore the critique.

Critics were initially troubled by the novel's bleak and ambiguous tone. Over time, scholars recognized its subversiveness—themes of "passing," racial fluidity, and parentage echo in literature and film. Adaptations have shifted in focus, sometimes emphasizing Roxy's agency, sometimes Wilson's detective role. Now, *Pudd'nhead Wilson* is seen as critical to understanding American attitudes on race, justice, and performance of identity.

Twain combines forensic innovation, emotional intensity, and biting satire, making *Pudd'nhead Wilson* a standout— its challenge to readers as urgent as ever.

The Mysterious Stranger—Philosophy, Religion, and Twain's Dark Vision

Late in life, Mark Twain's work grows darker. *The Mysterious Stranger* is his most probing investigation into meaning: a blend of philosophy, religion, and reality so entwined that certainty dissolves. Twain sets the tale in a remote Austrian village, haunted less by ghosts than by existential doubts. Into this insular world steps the enigmatic Satan—not the biblical tempter, but a radiant, cerebral being. Satan's logic is seductive—he entices the village boys into philosophical argument, exposing the fault lines in their moral certainty.

Dream and reality are indistinct; scenes jump in time, and villagers sometimes awaken unsure whether events happened or were dreams. This blending keeps both characters and readers on edge—what's real, what's imagined? Twain uses narrative uncertainty to challenge the very idea of truth.

Twain's critique of religion and morality is relentless. Satan's "Moral Sense" speech is pivotal—arguing that morality, supposedly a divine gift, is a source of misery and hypocrisy: "The Moral Sense teaches us what is right… but it also teaches us to do wrong, for gain or pleasure." Rituals are shown as hollow, prayers as rote, and forgiveness as self-interested. Through pointed dialogue, Twain mocks piety and exposes its brittleness.

The book's creation was as fractured as its narrative. Twain left several unfinished drafts. After he died, editors Albert Paine and Frederick Duneka patched together a publishable version, often changing Twain's intent. Archival evidence shows Twain's original vision as more despairing, ambiguous, and unresolved—mirroring his own deepening existential doubts.

Personal loss echoes in the novel's darkness. Twain suffered devastating grief in these years—his wife and two daughters died, as did many friends. In his letters, the humor dries up; he calls life "a grim jest." The novel's despair is thus rooted not just in philosophy, but in felt loss—there's no solace, only silence and unanswered questions.

Twain's vision aligns with philosophical pessimism, echoing Nietzsche's "death of God" and moral uncertainty. Yet an American skepticism persists—questioning progress and faith, seeking truth beneath optimism. Twain's late existential doubt feels intensely personal and singular.

The novel's questions remain unresolved: are humans mere playthings of a meaningless universe, or do we create our own purpose? Twain avoids easy closure. Satan embodies both liberty and nihilism—dispelling illusion, granting no hope. The novel's vision is bleak, but not empty: Twain urges acceptance of ambiguity and the perpetual search for meaning.

Archival research adds layers to interpretation: drafts reveal ongoing struggles with belief and despair. Ultimately, *The Mysterious Stranger* is far more than philosophical conjecture; it captures Twain wrestling with mortality, faith, and life's ultimate uncertainties.

Forgotten Treasures—Short Stories, Essays, and Unpublished Letters

Beyond his renowned novels, Twain's shorter works—stories, essays, letters—reveal his endless invention and keen insight. Too often neglected, these texts highlight Twain's relentless experimentation and ability to turn fresh eyes on human nature.

"Extracts from Adam's Diary" is a prime example of Twain's playful biblical satire. Adam, a bemused everyman, recounts awkward encounters with Eve. Humor grows from Adam's literalness and the repeated refrain: "It is curious," "I do not understand." Beneath the comedy are isolation, discovery, and the desire for connection—a meditation on misunderstanding and companionship.

Other works are more caustic. "The War Prayer" is Twain's most pointed political satire, written amidst U.S. military action but unpublished in his lifetime due to its severity. Twain describes a town praying for victory, interrupted by a stranger who insists that to pray for triumph is to pray for the suffering of others. Plain and forceful, the piece unmasks the violence beneath patriotic rhetoric. Though censored in his day, it remains a powerful warning about blind nationalism.

Twain's stories often satirize morality. In "The Facts Concerning the Recent Carnival of Crime in Connecticut," Twain meets his own conscience. The farce grows grim as he "murders" conscience for convenience—a biting depiction of self-deceit. Refrains like "I killed him with a chair" and "I felt better" lend dark comedy while probing honesty and justification.

"Advice to Little Girls" is an ironic guidebook, urging clever noncompliance and gentle subversion: be inventive in obedience; don't forgive easily. Twain's sharply concise counsel ("if you have...," "never allow...") undercuts adult authority and gender roles, fostering healthy skepticism.

Unpublished letters give us Twain's private voice. Discoveries reveal his vulnerabilities: in one, to his wife Olivia, he admits to frustration with criticism and fame's isolation; in another, he lampoons censors by inventing ridiculous bans. These missives, free of public posture, offer new views into Twain's psyche—his anxieties, friendships, and shifting allegiances.

Themes and methods from these briefer works echo in the novels. Satirical essays on law and justice prefigure courtroom scenes and narrative ironies elsewhere. Dialogues, refrains, and punchy rhythm in stories enliven longer fiction. Twain's persistent engagement with injustice, absurdity, and flawed virtue links pages across genres.

Ongoing research continues to reshape Twain's legacy. The Mark Twain Papers & Project finds drafts and manuscripts that challenge prior assumptions. Recent discoveries, like satirical fragments on Wall Street, show Twain's relentless refinement of both content and style. Each new letter or unfinished tale invites revised readings and insight, keeping his legacy alive and dynamic.

Twain's supposedly "minor" works are formidable in craft and insight, offering new angles on perennial themes: justice, absurdity, resilience. Rediscovered, these texts continue to surprise and deepen our understanding of his art. The quest for unpublished Twain material is itself a dynamic field, ensuring that even his overlooked writings can reshape the story of American letters.

Chapter 6: Behind the Curtain—Personal Struggles, Public Persona, and the Business of Being Twain

The Twain Family Circle—Love, Loss, and Domestic Life

Imagine a manuscript speckled with candle soot—the scent of ink and lavender lingering in Hartford's air. In that Victorian parlor, Mark Twain—Samuel Clemens—would read aloud new chapters, his wife, Olivia Langdon Clemens (Livy), listening thoughtfully. Their marriage, far from simple domesticity, was a nuanced partnership that molded every sentence Twain wrote. Their bond deepened through candid courtship letters, Twain playing Livy's "cavaliere servente"—humble and grateful, revealing ambition and wonder at her intellect ("Mark Twain's love letters," 1948). Years into marriage, Twain continued sending affectionate notes to Livy, especially during her long illnesses. Each scrap expressed enduring devotion and concern.

Livy's editorial role on Twain's work was profound. She read drafts closely, pruning excess and sharpening satire. Livy demanded clarity, questioning his tone and purpose when his words edged toward recklessness. Her marginalia—sometimes corrections, sometimes strong cautions—transformed rough comedy into prose capable of evoking both laughter and conscience. Publicly confident, Twain privately yearned for her approval, knowing her criticism sparked his best work. Their union also gave Twain entrance into Elmira's prominent Langdon family, securing social standing and connections to abolitionist circles. Nonetheless, he often felt like an outsider, always striving to prove worthy.

Life in the Hartford house balanced routine and exuberance. It was a lively, creative hub—rooms echoing with laughter, debate, and storytelling. Mornings featured family readings; evenings ended with poetry recitations or performances of Shakespeare. At dinner, conversation covered wide ground—politics, religion, art—with storytelling especially cherished, Twain spinning tales and prompting his children to find exaggerations or create alternate endings. Livy organized it all with warmth, guiding routines to nurture intellect without stifling curiosity.

With his children—Langdon, Susy, Clara, and Jean— Twain was both playful and protective. He wrote whimsical letters, illustrated notes, and elaborate bedtime stories. Beneath this levity was deep anxiety, intensified after the early death of his frail son Langdon. The infant's loss devastated both parents, haunting Twain, who blamed himself for not protecting his child ("Mark Twain's love letters," 1948).

Later, more grief visited the family. Susy's sudden death from meningitis shattered Twain, who described loss as "a dumb sense of vast loss," like losing a home to fire— stunned first, then realizing every irreplaceable thing is gone ("Mark Twain on a dumb sense of vast loss," 2015). Jean's epilepsy brought unpredictability and pain; her untimely death deepened Twain's helplessness. Olivia, too, was worn down by chronic illness. As Livy declined, Twain clung to hope—reading to her or sending notes when company was too much.

Financial Fiascos—Investments, Bankruptcy, and Global Lecture Tours

Twain's constant quest for financial security reveals a man never content to rely solely on royalties. He dove into risky investments with a gambler's urgency. Most notoriously, he poured his fortune into James Paige's complicated typesetting machine, which, despite initial promise, proved ill-timed and ultimately obsolete. Letters reveal his oscillation between hope and despair as these ventures drained his savings. Other failed bets—the Kaolotype photographic process, among them—left him further indebted, all in the hope of financial independence.

His eventual bankruptcy stemmed from bad luck and self-delusion. Shunning slow, steady gains, Twain's impatience and lack of bookkeeping left him exposed. Bankruptcy records show him battered by creditors; he apologized honestly in letters, making no excuses. Friends sometimes lent money, but debt kept mounting. Public humiliation was sharp—America's cleverest humorist was undone by business, not scandal.

To pay his debts, Twain launched arduous global lecture tours, recounted in "Following the Equator." He spoke night after night on multiple continents, masking exhaustion with satire. Illness and homesickness grew constant; only the determination to return debt-free kept him moving. Audience enthusiasm could not dispel his sense of isolation.

His turbulent finances reshaped his thoughts on wealth and the American Dream. Early on, he believed cleverness guaranteed riches, but experience led him to scorn both schemers and those chasing quick fortune. In letters and essays, Twain examined how optimism could curdle into delusion—failure stemmed as much from national myth as from individual shortcoming.

Twain's later writing critiques capitalist excess. He lampooned Gilded Age optimism and "progress," stuffing stories with failed inventors and broken investors. He pitied strivers but ripped into those who profited from others' failed hopes.

Thus, the randomness of fortune became a theme in his work. Though skeptically, he never wholly lost hope, and his private candor about this cycle echoes anyone burned by bad luck. Adversity became fodder for his stories, even when he made himself the punchline.

Grief and Creativity—How Tragedy Shaped Twain's Later Works

In his last decades, Twain endured nearly continual loss, clouding his public triumphs. The 1890s began well, but tragedy struck relentlessly. Susy's death from meningitis in 1896 shattered him; he described a life colored by absence and "dumb sense of vast loss." He grieved Jean, his epileptic daughter, after a sudden death in 1909, and Olivia's protracted illness and death left him unmoored. Twain's later writing reveals a man contending with emptiness, his public laughter shadowed by private anguish.

His journals and letters candidly recount mourning. Small daily reminders—an empty chair, an unfinished note—weighed heavily. To friends, Twain confided the recurring ache of grief, dreams of reunited loved ones dissolving into waking solitude. Even publicly, fatigue showed in his face.

After these losses, Twain's work grew somber and introspective. "The Death of Jean" is stark, raw pain laid bare, simply narrating events without consolation. Other late writings, such as "What Is Man?" and "Letters from the Earth," broadened into philosophical inquiry, questioning whether faith helps or deludes, probing meaning in suffering without offering comfort.

His late black humor, especially in "The Mysterious Stranger," depicted an indifferent universe—satire now pointed and unsparing. Laughter here comes from hard recognition, not sheer delight. Yet, brief lighter work suggests humor still offered some relief, however fleeting.

Twain's relationship with faith became fraught post-loss. Raised on scripture but often skeptical, death magnified his theological doubts. He sometimes longed for afterlife reunions, but more often found religious answers inadequate. He even joined séances—always curious but dubious.

Discussions with clergy revealed Twain's resistance to easy theological assurance. Still, he never fully surrendered hope—his late work mixed satire with flashes of tenderness, as lost daughters slipped into stories.

Ultimately, grief pushed him toward a starker honesty in both life and art. The optimism of his youth gave way to plain confrontation with pain, exposure of sentimentality, and a willingness to write unflinchingly of absence. His sorrow permanently changed his writing, the mark unmistakable.

Twain the Celebrity—Branding, Self-Promotion, and Media Savvy

Mark Twain's iconic white suit, unruly hair, and memorable mustache were not accidental—they were part of a deliberately crafted public image. Twain understood early on that appearance and persona communicated almost as much as words. The white suit, first worn later in life, instantly distinguished him; his rural drawl, honed for audiences, was as recognizable as his look. Through portraits, posters, and illustrations, Twain's image became universally recognizable.

He maximized every public appearance. Interviews became playful performances; he used humor to subvert questions and direct conversation, his quotable remarks (precursors of n-grams) designed for repetition and memorability.

On stage, Twain was more than an author—he performed, acting out stories and blending stand-up with satire. Touring posters announced his presence, his routines tailored to each city with local references, stories evolving to keep performances fresh and unique.

Twain navigated emerging mass media deftly. He fought for royalties and against publishing piracy, arguing for fair pay and copyright reforms—his negotiations set new standards for authors' rights. He licensed his name and image extensively, testing the border between literary prestige and merchandising.

As copyright laws changed, Twain advocated for protections for creative labor. His correspondence reveals tough negotiating, unafraid to reject unfair deals. These efforts helped set American writers on a firmer professional footing.

Fame, however, brought lampooning—his features caricatured by cartoonists. Twain, ever nimble, parodied himself to preempt others, using self-satire as both armor and spectacle.

The rewards of celebrity were real, but so was the scrutiny. Twain learned to surf public opinion, modifying his persona to sustain intrigue. Privately, he sometimes disliked his own image, but used the tension as performance, defying total comprehension.

Twain pioneered modern celebrity branding. His memorable phrases, signature look, and self-reinvention echo in today's media culture, where personal branding is common.

With a blend of humor and control, Twain ensured his legacy endures; every element—suit, story, smile—was calculated for the ages, previewing a world where everyone curates their brand.

Letters from the Edge—Private Writings and Revealing Diary Entries

Twain's private writings show greater vulnerability than his controlled public persona. In personal correspondence, sarcasm intensifies, bitterness appears, and disappointment is unvarnished. To friends, he vented about business betrayal, creditors, and bleak days, sometimes describing himself as "shipwrecked," unable to regain footing. These notes rarely resolved issues—Twain was frank about confusion, often leaving questions open.

Letters to his daughters, however, brimmed with invention and love, but during hardship, he wrote candidly about missing them or wishing to protect them. To Clara, he admitted loneliness, shifting from playful to confessional, showing that public laughter brought no private comfort.

Marginalia and diaries provide another perspective. Twain's handwritten notes to himself in manuscript margins are bluntly critical or questioning. During illness in the family, his entries grew terse and restless—tracking sleepless nights and distraction. When hope flickered, he expressed modest relief; if setbacks came, he recorded them without filter: "No change. Worse, if anything."

These fragments reveal the writing process behind Twain's stories: abandoned drafts, lists of titles, overheard phrases, stray jokes. Some scraps later became published pieces; others remained unfinished ideas.

Personal writings testify to resilience forged in solitude. Twain doubted his talent, obsessively revising for clarity and strength. Writing was therapy and discipline, both a means of finding form amid emotional disorder.

Their publication also raises ethical dilemmas. Twain mistrusted biography's reach, warning that stray papers could misrepresent him. Editors have to balance disclosure with contextualization—should a bitter remark written in illness be published? Does an incomplete fragment risk damaging the author's legacy?

Assembling Twain's inner life from these bits is both enlightening and fraught. There's candor—about regret, envy, flickers of hope—but also contradiction and ambivalence, thoughts trailed off unresolved. Memoir becomes a mosaic; diary a puzzle. Reading these, Twain transcends myth: a mind always in search, doubting, reaching for elusive meaning.

These writings form part of a lifelong internal dialogue—witty, humble, defiant—documenting an endless quest for truth, still compelling to this day.

Living with Contradiction—Humor, Depression, and Resilience

Twain's legendary humor disguised a private struggle deeper than his audiences realized. He oscillated between brilliance and bouts of despair—his friend William Dean Howells described Twain's smile as masking a "habitual sadness." After evenings of company and jokes, Twain often withdrew in silence, seldom sharing darker thoughts. Even his liveliest writings contained hints of self-doubt, proving that laughter and sadness often coexist.

Twain didn't shy away from discussing despair. He joked about suicide in such deadpan tones that listeners often laughed, missing the real pain underneath. His comic routines teetered on the edge of darkness; publicly, he likened survival to curiosity about the future, hinting that humor was more defense than escape. By making himself the joke, Twain controlled his narrative, disarming critics and owning his failures.

His writing often exaggerated his setbacks, transforming mishaps into anecdotes—lost investments became farcical stories, flops grew into lecture-circuit entertainment. This was Twain's way of reclaiming hardship. His speeches balanced cynicism and charm—laughing at humanity's folly one moment, foreshadowing disillusionment the next. Even so, there was resilience—a refusal to give up.

Twain's recovery strategy, familiar to many enduring depression, involved withdrawing from public life—traveling, taking up new projects, and then returning re-energized. This wasn't escapism, but a means of renewal. Returned, he plunged into new endeavors, whether books, essays, or public disputes, each disappointment triggering a reinvention.

This approach, accepting contradiction rather than fighting it, is perhaps his most lasting lesson. Twain admitted to inconsistencies and poked fun at himself, leaving behind enduring wisdom: "The secret of getting ahead is getting started," "Courage is resistance to fear—not absence of fear." These words, born of struggle, remain beloved for their insight.

Today's psychologists would recognize Twain's humor, reinvention, and connection to others as foundational resilience strategies. He anticipated modern notions of living with vulnerability and using storytelling to cope, echoes seen in many public figures today.

Twain's life offers a template for living with contradiction—recognizing sadness, still finding laughter; accepting imperfection, still searching for meaning. He showed resilience isn't about avoiding hardship, but facing it honestly and with wit. Each public appearance or new work was proof that humor could coexist with sorrow, making life not just bearable, but fully human.

This chapter reframes Twain not as an unreachable icon, but as someone who met adversity with honesty, invention, and steady effort. His journey reminds us all that even cultural giants wrestle with doubt—yet still shape works that inspire. Next, we'll explore how Twain's legacy continues to shape American writing and culture.

Chapter 7: Twain in Conversation—Friends, Foes, and the Literary Marketplace

Twain and the Literati—Emerson, Howells, and the Making of a Canon

Picture a Boston parlor on a rainy November evening: gas lamps flicker, cigar smoke curls, and Mark Twain's laugh stands out among New England's writers. These salons, more than idle gatherings, forged literary reputations and alliances, influencing the American canon. Twain leveraged these moments to define his standing among the country's literary giants, as friendships and debates shaped both his legacy and the development of national literature.

William Dean Howells, novelist, critic, and editor, played a critical role in Twain's rise from regional satirist to household name. After encountering *The Innocents Abroad* in 1869, Howells praised Twain's original style and insistence on lampooning both Americans and Europeans. His reviews and personal encouragement proved pivotal— at *The Atlantic Monthly*, Howells lobbied the traditional Boston establishment to embrace Twain's populist voice. Howells's feedback helped Twain hone his satire and deepen his themes while preserving his humor. Their long correspondence featured robust debate and genuine affection. As Ron Powers notes, without Howells's advocacy, Twain might have remained a local figure rather than achieving national stature.

Other literary relationships were more complex. Ralph Waldo Emerson, representing transcendentalist ideals, both inspired and challenged Twain. Emerson deemed Twain's humor "original," but hesitated at its irreverence and informality. Their interactions, marked by mixed praise and polite reservations, made Emerson a model of intellect for Twain but also someone whose abstraction he distrusted.

Henry James, renowned for psychological subtlety, also contrasted with Twain's directness. Twain publicly joked that James required a translator but conceded respect for his artistry. His quips masked an appreciation for the diversity James brought to American letters.

With Harriet Beecher Stowe, author of *Uncle Tom's Cabin*, Twain shared a mutual belief in literature's power to inspire change. Stowe was a regular guest in Twain's Hartford home—gatherings there blended lively debate on art, reform, and literary gossip, reinforcing camaraderie and engagement with urgent social issues.

Much of Twain's East Coast experience centered on *The Atlantic Monthly* circle, where he mingled with luminaries like Holmes, Lowell, and Howe. Always the outsider, Twain defied European modes and Boston decorum, using biting satire to challenge the group's conventions. Over time, his wit won reluctant admiration.

Twain's rivalry with Bret Harte, another writer steeped in Western vernacular, exemplified productive tension. Contrast in stylistic temperament made their collaborations engaging, while correspondence—sometimes harsh, sometimes fond—raised both men's literary game. Harte admired Twain's ability to transform common speech into art, while Twain appreciated Harte's meticulous attention to place and detail.

Howells's support was essential for Twain's acceptance into the literary canon. He convinced publishers and critics that Twain's humor was grounded in social realism and sharp observation, not mere entertainment. Emerson's measured praise helped broaden Twain's appeal among academics and more conservative readers, while endorsements from prominent writers lent legitimacy to Twain's experiments with dialect and satire.

Through advocacy, rivalry, and collaboration, Twain both gained entry to the literary elite and helped redefine American literary boundaries.

Feuds, Fights, and Friendships—Twain's Public Spats and Private Alliances

Mark Twain's standing as a literary titan was forged through confrontation as well as consensus. He dueled in print, sparred with rivals, and weaponized his wit. His most memorable feuds were performances, not merely shows of ego, but calculated acts to stake out new territory in American letters. Twain often targeted entrenched figures—like James Russell Lowell—lampooning their archaic prose and shattering their authority. Twain's barbs were tactical: challenging gatekeepers and advocating for humor and plain speech in literature.

French critic Paul Bourget, who disparaged American society, prompted Twain to reply with a searing satirical essay, parodying Bourget's condescension and highlighting the flaws in his arguments. Twain's feuds always played to the audience—whether fellow writers or the public—and his disregard for critical orthodoxy made him impossible to ignore.

His friendship with, and later rivalry against, Bret Harte was public and painful. Early admiration gave way to open ridicule—over both art and finances. Twain mocked Harte's supposed laziness, airing grievances in letters and on stage. Even at his harshest, Twain preferred humor over insult, knowing laughter could wound deeper than anger.

Twain's mock critique, "Fenimore Cooper's Literary Offenses," skewered Cooper's storytelling with mock seriousness, listing supposed narrative blunders in biting prose. The essay exemplifies Twain's approach: devastating literary criticism as public spectacle. He frequently adopted pseudonyms or alter-egos, shifting tone or escalating attacks without revealing personal animosity, maintaining a sense of playful ambiguity.

Yet Twain was not just contentious; he was capable of sustaining deep friendships. His bond with Joseph Twichell, a Hartford minister, endured through hardship and personal loss. Their letters reveal a warmth that contrasts with Twain's public facade, cemented by long walks and candid debate. Twichell offered faith and counsel when Twain faltered.

His partnership with Charles Dudley Warner, co-authoring "The Gilded Age," combined sharp satire with social critique. Warner's even-handedness tempered Twain's exuberance, yielding a richer narrative than either might have crafted alone. Their creative friction produced lasting work.

Alliances influenced Twain's creative process and reputation. Friends edited drafts, provided themes, and sometimes facilitated deals. Private debates often sparked new tales or arguments. Even reconciliations after public feuds attracted attention, enhancing Twain's stature in the literary rumor mill.

Twain didn't hesitate to fictionalize former friends or foes, transforming adversaries into universal examples of folly, ambition, or pretense, blurring the line between life and fiction.

His public image—irreverent yet principled—emerged from these cycles of rivalry and friendship. Twain understood that audiences craved both scandal and substance. Every clash or alliance added texture to his mythic persona: outspoken outsider and steadfast friend.

The Business of Authorship—Contracts, Censorship, and Copyright Battles

Twain approached writing as a business—a realm demanding vigilance and negotiation. When facing publishers, he insisted on controlling his work's fate, leading him to found Charles L. Webster & Co. This venture gave Twain unprecedented agency: he secured better royalties and dictated artistic decisions, particularly for *Adventures of Huckleberry Finn*. He worked closely with illustrator E.W. Kemble, providing detailed direction to maintain consistency with his prose's tone. Business, not sentiment, defined these partnerships.

Money drove Twain, but so did fairness. He fought for percentages over flat fees, insisting compensation accurately reflected sales. Advances became battlegrounds; Twain would not surrender manuscripts unless terms recognized his commercial worth.

His business acumen extended to legal policy. Copyright, for Twain, shielded authors from pirates and plagiarists. He lobbied for reform, standing before Congress and writing in the *North American Review*. International copyright treaties became his cause—Twain led the movement for fair compensation in a borderless market.

Twain's books, notably *Huckleberry Finn*, also attracted controversy and censorship. When the Concord Public Library banned it in 1885, debate erupted about obscenity and respectability. Critics objected to its language and frankness about race and authority. Twain, in turn, used the attention to call out hypocrisy and promote sales, though public censure stung.

Market realities shaped Twain's creative choices. Serialization built anticipation, and book-agent subscriptions widened reach, democratizing literature. Twain's method required vigilance against fraud but expanded readership. To appeal to broader audiences (and wary publishers), Twain sometimes toned down dialects or softened scenes, lamenting betrayals of his artistic vision. However, he recognized that compromise could be necessary for staying in print and expanding impact.

Twain always embraced his dual identity: writer and businessman. He believed profit proved literature mattered beyond train stations and review pages. Each negotiation modeled an author's right to dignity—a struggle that anticipates today's debates over royalties and creative control.

Twain Abroad—Global Influence and Encounters with European Elites

Twain quickly moved beyond the Mississippi, becoming America's best-known literary ambassador in Europe. His overseas tours were more than book events—they were chances to test American humor against Old World traditions. Twain was welcomed in London as a symbol of new-world irreverence, dazzling the English court (and Queen Victoria) with his trademark white suit and self-assurance.

In Paris, Twain engaged with literary salons, finding the French appreciative but wary of his bluntness. He challenged pretension with tales of Missouri and California, bridging cultures through laughter. Sparring with foreign critics, he insisted literature should both amuse and enlighten, and left convinced that storytelling could transcend borders.

Correspondence and encounters with European celebrities mattered as much as awards. Twain's rapport with Rudyard Kipling—who admired Twain and sought his counsel—was shaped by thoughtful letters and debates over colonialism, language, and storytelling. Their exchanges clarified both men's roles in shaping modern English-language fiction.

In England, Twain's meeting with George Bernard Shaw yielded dialogues charged with wit and critique—Twain admired Shaw's fearlessness, Shaw his truth-telling charm. In Russia, Twain found himself among fans of Leo Tolstoy; while they never met, discussions with Tolstoy's circle explored shared skepticism toward authority and the social role of satire.

Travel shaped Twain's views on culture and class. His travelogues, especially "The Innocents Abroad," lampooned both American tourists and European customs, poking fun at credulous travelers and guarded guides alike. He questioned both "civilization" and the promises of American democracy, attentive to how ritual and hierarchy shaped human behavior.

These transatlantic experiences amplified Twain's reputation. London newspapers hailed his originality but bristled at irreverence. International adaptations of his work abounded, making his themes accessible from Berlin stages to Parisian classrooms and Russian critical circles.

His zenith abroad came with Oxford's honorary degree in 1907, a global headline event. Twain's informal attire and speech at the ceremony symbolized the fusion of national identity and literary influence that defined his international stature.

Encounters with writers and dignitaries deepened Twain's belief in literature as a cross-cultural conversation. Exposure to Europe's salons and hierarchies sharpened his ideas on satire, democracy, and the potential of storytelling free from convention.

Twain as Mentor and Model—Influencing New Generations of Writers

Twain's influence extended well past his novels—he served as mentor, correspondent, and endorser for a rising generation of American writers. His letters to emerging authors mixed encouragement, practical feedback, and humor. Helen Keller benefited directly—Twain vouched for her with publishers, advising her to trust her judgment above critics. He encouraged Upton Sinclair, offering critique without pretension and providing public endorsements when requested.

Twain's example—theming skepticism toward authority, celebrating vernacular speech, and equating humor with critique—became foundational for American realism and regionalism. Writers like Willa Cather and Sherwood Anderson drew upon Twain's willingness to depict ordinary people authentically. The influence is also clear in Ring Lardner's wry stories and Dorothy Parker's wit—each channeling Twain's spirit of plainspoken, incisive observation.

Modern novelists, including Hemingway and Toni Morrison, have credited Twain as the source of a distinct American voice and narrative freedom. Hemingway stated that all modern American literature descends from *Huckleberry Finn*, while Morrison highlighted Twain's demonstration that dialect can reveal emotional and social truth.

Direct interventions strengthened Twain's legacy. He advised Franklin Sanborn, urging clarity and brevity, assisted Hartford journalists with revision advice, and advocated for reporters to both inform and entertain—principles many carried through long careers.

Twain's support extended into publishing: letters to agents and editors helped secure contracts for deserving young authors, reflecting his urge that literature stay responsive to new voices. His hands-on criticism ranged from pointed notes on style to broader life lessons—urging honesty, courage, and tactful use of offense and laughter.

Twain's presence set a model: humor with purpose, outsider perspective with authority. Later generations respected his willingness to question, to satirize society and himself.

His legacy persists: in punchy columns, voice-driven novels, and tales finding wisdom in rebellion. His advice—to trust observation over received wisdom—still guides honest writing about the world today.

The Critics' Chorus—Contemporary Reviews and Evolving Reputations

Twain's books drew mixed reactions—delight from some, concern or confusion from others. Leading periodicals disagreed on whether *Huckleberry Finn* marked a new era in storytelling or breached literary decorum with its dialect and irreverence. *A Connecticut Yankee in King Arthur's Court* received similarly polarized feedback—praise for sharp wit, criticism for biting satire, and genre blending. These divergent reviews affected how publishers promoted Twain: as a rebel or as a respectable artist, depending on the moment.

His critical reputation evolved after his death. Early twentieth-century scholarship saw him mainly as an entertainer rather than a "serious" author. This changed by mid-century: critics like Lionel Trilling hailed *Huckleberry Finn* as a unique exploration of American complexity. T.S. Eliot placed Twain within the great tradition, acknowledging the roughness but affirming its importance. Toni Morrison later re-examined Twain's work, focusing on race and voice and inviting readers to encounter discomfort as well as hope.

Debate continues: since the 1950s, *Huckleberry Finn* has sparked public and school board disputes over its content. Some object to language and themes; others argue against erasing difficult history. Censorship debates flare in media and meetings, as education policies adapt with each generation's priorities.

Teaching approaches have shifted: educators now treat Twain's novels as documents for honest discussion about language, power, and belonging. Some pair Twain with contemporary writers, others guide students through context and controversy. Literary anthologies and institutions enshrine Twain's status, but selection and interpretation remain contested.

Outside academia, awards like the Mark Twain Prize and museum exhibitions continually refresh his image, acknowledging humor and social critique as his legacy. Centennial events draw both scholars and fans, reminding us that reputations are always in flux.

Twain's critical journey reflects the nation's struggle to define itself—pride, anxiety, laughter, and discomfort intertwining. His works force readers to confront their past and present with honesty, wit, and restless questioning.

The following chapter turns to how Twain's writing keeps sowing debate—shaping both literature and wider discussions on justice, memory, and belonging.

Chapter 8: Twain's Living Legacy—Controversy, Influence, and the Future of American Satire

Twain in the Classroom—Pedagogy, Censorship, and the Canon Wars

Imagine a high school classroom where the teacher reads from "Adventures of Huckleberry Finn." Some students are engaged; others are visibly uneasy, as Twain's words press on ongoing debates about curriculum, teaching, and cultural values.

Twain entered American classrooms early in the twentieth century. "The Adventures of Tom Sawyer" was embraced for its humor, lively youth, and broad appeal, making it popular with readers and teachers. By the 1930s and 1940s, "Huckleberry Finn" cemented its place in high school and college syllabi, praised for its realism and its portrayal of life on the Mississippi. Literature ascended post–World War II as a means to understand society, positioning Twain among the American "classics." Yet as education diversified in the late twentieth century, scrutiny over his works increased.

Teaching Twain today is both rewarding and challenging. His novels spark critical thinking—encouraging students to question power, recognize hypocrisy, and explore race and class. Reaping these benefits, however, requires care. Twain's use of racial slurs, dialects, and stereotypes still shocks, potentially distressing especially marginalized students. For instance, reading "Huck Finn" aloud distressed African American students in one New Jersey district, prompting parental concern and debate about curriculum. Educators now contextualize Twain's language and era, using historical background and discussion rather than evasion.

Student reactions to Twain are diverse. For some, humor and irreverence offer engagement; for others, his words are barriers. Classes often debate whether Huck's moral growth offsets language use or whether Jim inspires empathy or reinforces stereotypes. Such dialogue is valuable but relies on classroom trust and good facilitation—not always attainable in every community.

Censorship still shadows Twain's work. U.S. school boards have periodically removed "Huckleberry Finn," citing offensive language and perpetuated racism. Parents protest; teachers worry about student welfare. In Cherry Hill, New Jersey, notable distress led to the novel's temporary removal and mandatory historical training for teachers. The resulting debate exposed divisions: some saw bans as an erasure of important history, others viewed the novel's language as indefensible in modern classrooms.

These disputes reflect broader "canon wars"—should the curriculum favor certain works and, if so, which? Since the 1970s, critics have questioned what gets included and why, and whether inclusion should be more diverse. Twain's defenders see him as critiquing injustice and open dialogue about national history; critics argue that his works can perpetuate prejudice and cause harm

Schools have adapted. Some offer students a choice between "Huckleberry Finn" and, for example, books by Toni Morrison or Jacqueline Woodson, privileging conversation over prescription. Others use guides framing Twain within discussions of race, power, and language, or invite guest speakers to offer a perspective on problematic passages.

Race, Language, and Modern Critique—Reading Twain in the 21st Century

Twain's writing persists, repeatedly sparking debate—especially about race and language. "Adventures of Huckleberry Finn" returns to prominence as critics assess its literary strength and discomfort. Recent essays position Twain as both a product and critic of his era's prejudices. Some applaud his exposure of America's hypocrisies and engagement with racism; others say his satire sometimes falters, inflicting harm. Central is the question: can well-intentioned literature still wound readers? Modern critics ask: Does literature illuminate or perpetuate pain?

Language is at the core. Twain's repeated use of racial slurs remains contentious. Educators and readers dispute addressing, softening, or removing these words. When NewSouth Books published an edition of "Huckleberry Finn" replacing the N-word with "slave," debate flared. Proponents felt it preserved classroom access while sparing trauma; opponents saw it as erasing history and diminishing the original's power. Comparing versions reveals how a single word shapes tone, character dynamics, and historical perception: the original confronts racism, while the cleaned version increases accessibility but may erase context and challenge. Literature thus becomes a battleground: should it comfort, disturb, or both? Modern printings now include glosses and essays—guiding readers through this tension.

Contemporary writers and artists actively engage Twain's legacy. Toni Morrison, writing about "Huckleberry Finn," reinterprets the novel as grappling with conscience—insisting that Twain's flawed yet groundbreaking portrayal of Jim forces readers to face reality rather than evade it. Today, writers of color often feel ambivalence: some appreciate attempts to humanize Jim and critique white culture, while others highlight restrictions—Jim's story too often mediated by Huck. Interviews with modern authors reveal a range of responses, from admiration to critique.

In classrooms, students try "updating" Twain—reimagining Jim's ending, adding new voices, or constructing projects that highlight gaps in Twain's America. A popular exercise involves rewriting scenes from Jim's viewpoint, exposing both empathy and erasure. Some debate whether satire remains effective if language's potential to harm endures.

New scholarship broadens engagement with Twain. The Mark Twain Project Online annotates dialect, slang, and context, encouraging readers to slow down and reconsider. Digital humanities provide interactive maps, timelines, and guides showing Twain's stories intersecting with legal, racial, and historical realities.

Public humanities further these conversations. Community groups host forums facing Twain's contradictions. Libraries pair Twain with modern replies—poems, essays, art—that critique or answer him. Annotated texts now include voices previously marginalized—Indigenous critics on land and erasure, Black scholars on trauma and hope in Huck and Jim.

Technology revolutionizes engagement with Twain. E-books let readers trace recurring themes and words, revealing textual patterns previously hidden. Switching between editions or linking the novel with a broader context is now simple.

No longer is the question whether to read Twain, but how and whose voices matter. His texts test how society debates history, language, empathy, and memory. Every generation brings unique questions—defining not only Twain's aims, but how his words affect readers today: provoking, unsettling, inspiring action, or demanding reconsideration.

Twain on Stage and Screen—Adaptations, Parodies, and Cultural Afterlives

Twain's stories reach beyond books, shaping movies, television, theater, and even comics. "Adventures of Huckleberry Finn" has spawned numerous adaptations, each transforming Huck and Jim for a new era. Early silent films highlighted slapstick—the raft trip and Tom's mischief—while later versions addressed darker themes with varying candor. Disney's 1993 "The Adventures of Huck Finn" softened the harsher elements for family viewers, but lost critical social commentary. Other adaptations, like Michael Curtiz's 1960 version, attempted to balance innocence with brutality, using natural settings and dialects to evoke Twain's spirit. Each adaptation reflects contemporary values—be it postwar hope, civil rights unrest, or modern quests for authenticity.

On stage, the musical "Big River" combined bluegrass and gospel to elevate Jim's perspective, imbuing new emotional force. Theater's intimacy fostered a close, immediate bond with Huck and Jim, with music amplifying longing and hope. Garnering praise and awards, "Big River" introduced Twain anew to those outside his readership.

Twain's influence flourishes in parody and creative remixes. Artists and writers borrow his characters and style for humor, commentary, or both. "Tom Sawyer, Detective" parodies detective fiction, letting Tom outwit adults with youthful logic. Contemporary authors, like Jon Clinch, reimagine Twain's universe (as in "Finn"), pushing original themes darker. Graphic novels place Huck, Tom, and Becky into steampunk or supernatural roles—blending nostalgia and creativity, echoing Twain's penchant for exaggeration. Cartoons and young adult works channel his voice, irreverence, and questioning spirit.

Twain himself is iconic. Impersonators in white suits and wild wigs wear his drawl in classrooms and on TV. Hal Holbrook's "Mark Twain Tonight!" didn't just deliver Twain's words, but embodied him for decades—shaping public imagination. This tradition continues in animation, such as "The Adventures of Mark Twain," which carried viewers on surreal journeys through his tales, mixing whimsy and melancholy for children.

Popular culture constantly reimagines Twain. He appears in commercials, selling goods with humor and Americana. Comics and memes match him with presidents or pop icons. Lookalikes judge school events or debate students—carrying Twain's wit, skepticism, and common sense into daily life.

Adaptation invites debate: does change compromise Twain's essence? Directors and writers differ—some insist on fidelity; others prioritize contemporary resonance. Purists criticize updates that downplay historical challenges, finding them diluted. Others defend change, arguing that stories evolve best when refreshed. Creators range from those keeping the period's flavor to ones concentrating on the emotional core; some recast Jim as the protagonist, seeing reimagining as truest to Twain's rebellious streak.

Reactions range. Some newer versions are praised for honoring complexity; others are dismissed for glossing over nuance or being too restrained. Scholars scrutinize new interpretations while wary of oversimplification; audiences discuss authenticity post-performance or online.

Adaptation means confronting Twain's legacy—treating what endures with care, while allowing each era to reinterpret whitewashed fences, riverbanks, and raft escapes for themselves. Twain's ongoing presence proves satire, curiosity, and moral struggle remain evergreen, always reinvented for new voices and stages.

Twain's Heirs—Tracing His Influence on Modern Humorists and Satirists

Twain's style is deeply woven into modern American humor, satire, and storytelling. Writers mix vernacular and eloquence, using plain speech to deliver sharp, funny insights—transforming mundane mishaps into stories that both sting and amuse. Kurt Vonnegut stands out among Twain's heirs, openly crediting Twain's deadpan style and sharp commentary as vital influences. In "Slaughterhouse-Five" and "Cat's Cradle," the narrator wryly catalogues absurdity, urging readers to find the hurt beneath humor. Vonnegut lauded Twain's bravery in confronting cruelty, using laughter to engage with difficult truths—a strategy that shaped countless writers.

Lorrie Moore channels Twain's sensibility in her fiction through deadpan wit and irony. Her compressed sentences and precise humor uncover everyday heartbreak, always hinting at the pain beneath. Like Twain, she trusts readers to sense both the mirth and sorrow intertwined in real lives—her characters deliver truth through awkward humor, never straying far from genuine emotion. In Moore's stories, the "tall tale" exposes realities in life's odd turns.

Twain's signature—drawn from vernacular speech, wild tales, and pointed satire—resonates in George Saunders and Dave Eggers. Saunders crafts surreal worlds using the everyday American idiom, pushing reality into the bizarre much as Twain did. Saunders' unvarnished voice blurs real and absurd, always questioning what can be believed. Eggers, in "A Heartbreaking Work of Staggering Genius," fuses confession with parody, irony with earnestness—mirroring Twain's knack for blending memoir and creative invention. Both writers favor familiar words and structures, then twist expectations to surprise.

Sarah Vowell, known for comic history essays and radio, invokes Twain in combining irreverence and deep research. Her playful tone and layered facts recall Twain's travel writing—serious, yet never solemn. Vowell punctures self-importance without losing sight of serious themes beneath the comedy.

Twain's influence also appears on stage and screen. Jon Stewart, on "The Daily Show," echoed Twain's voice, skewering politicians with short, sharp sentences. Stewart's direct address mimicked Twain's strategy: mocking authority to provoke thought. Stephen Colbert adopted a character parodying punditry, reflecting Twain's method of exposing foolishness by acting it. Comedians, with wry smiles, question power—walking Twain's path.

The Mark Twain Prize for American Humor traces these connections, awarding those who shape national dialogue through comedy. Recipients such as Richard Pryor, Tina Fey, and Dave Chappelle use humor to reveal truths and promote change. Stand-up performers today rework Twain's themes—lampooning hypocrisy, exposing the gulf between ideal and reality, and mining comedy from hardship. Chris Rock and Hannah Gadsby, among others, dissect politics, balancing pain and punchlines.

Twain's global influence is notable. Salman Rushdie cited Twain's effect on "Midnight's Children"—using magical realism to challenge imperial histories with humor. In Japan, manga and anime adaptations bring "Tom Sawyer" and "Huck Finn" to young audiences, retaining the spirit of rebellion and wit.

All these heirs—novelists, comics, essayists worldwide— draw from Twain's well: ordinary speech shaped into satire, empathy layered with laughter, tales that reveal hard truths. His legacy flows through their work, subtle or overt—a persistent river running toward new shores.

Critical Debates—Ethics, Empathy, and the Limits of Satire

Twain's sharpest satire reveals more than comedy—it unveils complexity: mockery, discomfort, and, at times, unexpected kindness. Scholars and readers still debate: where does satirical critique end and ethical responsibility begin? Twain's harshest jokes—targeting politicians, clergy, or neighbors—balance exposing folly and causing harm. "The Awful German Language" hilariously skewers grammar but risks offense. Meanwhile, "The Facts Concerning the Recent Carnival of Crime in Connecticut" turns the lampoon on Twain himself. Yet, as an animal advocate, he set humor aside—calling vivisection an "infamy"—demonstrating satirists can champion direct empathy.

Twain's satire is potent when humor yields to pathos. Late in "Huckleberry Finn," farce gives way to Huck's moral reckoning—his choice to help Jim escapes irony. Likewise, "The Tragedy of Pudd'nhead Wilson" shifts from comic bewilderment to a somber reflection on race and destiny. Twain lures readers in with laughter, then reveals the suffering beneath, showing satire's power to harm and to heal, depending on how it's used and received.

Today, debates about satire's limits are heightened by social media. Now, what once circulated quietly can go viral with context lost. A single tweet or joke may trigger outrage or boycotts. Recent controversies over comedians' "punching down" echo old anxieties: Does satire challenge intolerance or reinforce it? Twain encountered such backlash; now, consequences come faster, and debates can be reduced to soundbites.

Modern writers and performers tread cautiously. Some believe satire must unsettle to provoke reflection. Others, wary in a polarized era, argue that even well-intentioned humor can injure or marginalize. Recent cases include books pulled after online protest, comedians confronted after provocative sets, and calls for balancing wit and sensitivity. Twain's dilemmas resurface: does satire merely reflect society's flaws, or perpetuate them? When does mockery become cruelty?

Classrooms and activist circles turn satire into discussion. Students ask if Twain's humor still works or if boundaries are needed. Some argue context is everything—a joke alarming to one era may constructively challenge another. Others say that if a joke wounds, intent matters little. Current satirists are split: some follow Twain's irreverence in challenging authority, while others soften their approach for empathy's sake.

Subtle discussion is crucial, but rare. In class, students analyze "Huck Finn" to question whether it lampoons racism or embeds it—a snapshot of divides across society. Critics weigh benefits and risks, using theory, ethics, and personal experience. Public debates often question whether Twain's barbs injure too deeply or provide comfort in adversity.

Digital media both amplifies and complicates these debates. Satire spreads beyond authorial intent, interpreted through readers' backgrounds and assumptions. Small language shifts can tip tone from catharsis to harm. This continual negotiation keeps Twain's relevance alive: satire as a lively conversation about power, empathy, and the truth's boundaries.

Twain was both a ruthless satirist and an advocate for the vulnerable, proving satire's complexity—it can expose and deepen injustice. Readers and writers face an enduring challenge not only to laugh or recoil, but to reflect: whose pain is affected, whose story traded, whose humanity acknowledged?

Collecting Twain—Archives, Artifacts, and the Ongoing Quest for Discovery

Step inside the Mark Twain House & Museum in Hartford, and you enter a living archive. Walls echo with stories, and display cases present Twain's possessions: furniture, portraits, annotated manuscripts, and letters to friends and rivals. Each room reveals a side of Twain's creativity, loss, or ambition. Curators reconstruct his habits and peculiarities, often from scrawls and margins—each detail revealing his thought process. For both fans and scholars, this museum links legend to life.

Hartford, however, is only part of a network. The Mark Twain Papers at the University of California, Berkeley, house perhaps the richest collection—drafts, marginalia, correspondence, and artifacts. Archivists preserve fragile materials, continually expanding as new items surface privately or through donation. Unexpected finds—a lost letter, an early draft—can stir excitement and even alter scholarly understanding or interpretation.

Discovery is painstaking but rewarding. Sometimes a trunk at an estate sale holds annotated Twains or notes on envelopes, sending waves through literary circles. Auctions of Twain memorabilia—first editions or personal effects— ignite bidding wars, their cultural worth plainly exceeding monetary value. When an edited "Tom Sawyer" surfaces, it's more than a book—it's shared history. Physical artifacts, like pipes or glasses, raise questions about public versus private stewardship—should all be broadly accessible, or is there value in passionate guardianship by collectors? Such debates recur as institutions compete for significant artifacts while seeking loans or gifts.

Technology has revolutionized access. Digitization at Berkeley and elsewhere lets anyone view Twain's handwritten notes online. Interactive archives allow side-by-side comparisons of drafts, tracing story evolution. Virtual tours of the Hartford house bring Twain's environment to any home. Social media distributes "Twainiana"—rare artifacts, photos, oddities—sparking new interest among readers who may not have read his books.

Crowdsourcing invites fans to participate—transcribing letters or identifying figures in old photographs—giving preservation a collaborative dimension. These projects inject fresh enthusiasm, creating a dynamic, growing digital archive available to all.

At the intersection of culture and commerce, debates continue: do high prices for literary artifacts benefit or hinder public access? Newsworthy sales of Twain's writing desk or a lock of hair stir reflection about what it means to "own" history. Some claim museums provide irreplaceable context; others affirm private collectors are essential to conserving artifacts. Each artifact shapes our memory of Twain and influences how he is studied and remembered.

As this chapter closes, it's clear that memory is preserved by many hands: curators, collectors, scholars, and fans share in sustaining Twain's legacy. Discovery itself guarantees his works continue to inspire imagination and inquiry. Next, we shift from preservation to reflection: what does it mean, today, to keep returning to and rethinking Mark Twain?

Conclusion

You have now traveled the winding roads and restless waters of Mark Twain's life and work. You have met a boy peering at steamboats from the muddy banks of the Mississippi, a young man chasing fortune out West, a writer whose wit cut through the noise of the Gilded Age, and a public figure who wore a white suit as both armor and invitation. If you take one thing from this journey, let it be this: Twain remains at the heart of American literature not because he was always right or always kind, but because he was always searching—questioning, laughing, grieving, and never content with easy answers. His wit, empathy, and complexity make his voice impossible to silence and just as impossible to ignore.

Throughout this book, we have traced the major themes that shaped Twain's legacy. You have seen how his Missouri childhood—marked by riverbanks, feuds, poverty, and the complex voices of neighbors—gave him his first lessons in storytelling and social critique. You have followed him into the peril and promise of steamboat piloting, where risk and resilience became second nature. The West tested his hopes and sharpened his satire, giving him the tools to turn hardship into humor. We examined how his mastery of dialect and deadpan delivery reshaped the very sound of American writing and how his fierce gaze exposed the deceptions of power and the follies of progress in a gilded age. We took a close look at both his best-known works—*Tom Sawyer*, *Huckleberry Finn*, *A Connecticut Yankee*—and those that deserve more attention, like *Pudd'nhead Wilson* and his incisive essays and letters. In each chapter, we have seen the pull between Twain's public fame and private doubts, his complicated friendships and feuds, and the swirl of praise, criticism, and controversy that continues to follow his name.

What should you carry forward from Twain's story? First, a more nuanced understanding of his genius and his flaws. Twain was a master of humor, but he was also a careful observer of pain and injustice. His jokes often revealed deeper wounds. By reading him with attention to context—his time, his place, his personal struggles—you begin to see why his laughter could not exist without his sorrow. You also gain practical strategies for reading his work: look for the "wink" in his stories, the places where he lets you in on the joke or invites you to judge for yourself. Recognize how he used dialect to capture the rhythms of real speech, and how he borrowed from the everyday to make lasting art. Let his sharp social critique challenge you to question the stories your own culture tells.

Twain's contradictions are not flaws to be ignored, but clues to his humanity. He battled loss and financial ruin. He faced criticism from friends and strangers alike. He was both an insider and an outsider, a beloved public figure and a man who often felt alone. His life reminds us that greatness is not a matter of perfection, but of persistence and honesty. Twain's willingness to confront his own errors, to mourn his losses openly, and to revise his thinking makes him not just a writer to admire, but a person to learn from.

I have strived in these pages to give you a balanced account—to praise Twain's courage and creativity, but also to confront the difficult parts of his legacy. The controversies around race, gender, and language in his work demand thoughtful reading. It is not enough to celebrate Twain's boldness without acknowledging the pain some of his words can still cause. You can honor his intention to speak truth by facing these challenges directly, using them as opportunities for honest conversation in your reading and teaching.

Twain's influence runs through today's literature, humor, and social commentary. Writers and comedians still borrow from his style and spirit. His empathy for outsiders, his willingness to poke holes in the powerful, and his restless curiosity live on in the best of American culture. When you listen to a stand-up comic skewer politicians, or read a novelist who dares to use the language of real people, you hear echoes of Twain. His spirit of questioning is not just part of literary history; it is alive in every debate about who gets to tell America's story and how.

But Twain's legacy is not something to admire from afar. It is a living thing, open to your own discovery and interpretation. I urge you to keep exploring. Seek out annotated editions that add new context to his works. Visit a museum, or explore the Mark Twain Papers online to see his drafts and letters for yourself. Join a reading group or class, or simply share your thoughts with a friend. Every new perspective adds to the conversation. Twain's story is not finished—and your voice matters in shaping what it means.

As you reflect on what you have learned, I invite you to challenge your own assumptions about Twain, about literature, and about the stories that shape our understanding of the past. Share what you have discovered here with others. Ask questions. Argue. Laugh. A classic author is not a relic, but a companion for the journey—a source of insight, trouble, and, above all, conversation.

My own motivation for writing this book is simple. I have seen too many readers turned away by myths or misunderstandings about Twain—believing him to be out of reach, too old-fashioned, or too controversial to matter. My goal is to help you overcome those barriers and find, in Twain's work, a guide and a challenge for your own life. Thank you for joining me in this search for the real Mark

Twain. Your curiosity, patience, and willingness to wrestle with complexity have brought these pages to life.

Now, I urge you: Take Twain's curiosity and critical thinking with you. Whether you are reading, teaching, or simply talking about books, let his example sharpen your questions and deepen your appreciation for the voices of the past. Help others see that classic authors deserve not blind reverence, but honest engagement. In doing so, you help keep the conversation alive—not just about Twain, but about who we are, what we value, and how we tell our own stories.

Twain taught us that laughter and inquiry belong together— that a nation's conscience can be shaped as much by its humor as by its laws. Carry that lesson forward, and you will find that the river of American literature, like the Mississippi, is still wide, deep, and waiting for new navigators.

Why Twain Endures: The Language of Freedom

Every generation rediscovers Twain because he represents freedom: freedom of speech, freedom of thought, freedom of storytelling. His language is rebellious but warm, rebellious but humane. He invites readers not just to witness America but to *talk* it, to embrace the messy, vibrant, hilarious voice of the nation. Twain's linguistic legacy is not a style—it is an attitude.

Thank you for completing this book.

I hope its contents meant a lot to you. As I mentioned earlier, when you can, please spend just a little time writing a review of *Mark Twain And The Making of American Literature*

Many potential readers consider the quality and quantity of reviews a book has earned, and the better the reviews, the more a seller prioritizes it.

All you have to do is locate this book online, scroll down to where it says "Write a customer review," and follow the directions to write a much-appreciated review. It doesn't have to be long. They recommend at least a few sentences.

Thanks much in advance.

Please keep reading,

Blake Whitworth

References

- *How Mark Twain's Childhood Influenced His Literary Works* https://www.biography.com/authors-writers/mark-twain-early-life-facts
- *The Adventures of the Real Tom Sawyer* https://www.smithsonianmag.com/history/the-adventures-of-the-real-tom-sawyer-35894722/
- *Local Color and Regionalism (Chapter 7) - Mark Twain in ...* https://www.cambridge.org/core/books/mark-twain-in-context/local-color-and-regionalism/01E58A6F64B588CE91FB53B2BB98A41B
- *Mark Twain, the Blood-Feud, and the South* https://www.jstor.org/stable/20077424
- *Mark Twain receives steamboat pilot's license | April 9, 1859* https://www.history.com/this-day-in-history/april-9/mark-twain-receives-steamboat-pilots-license
- *Dialects in The Adventures of Huckleberry Finn* https://papersowl.com/examples/dialects-in-the-adventures-of-huckleberry-finn/
- *Mark Twain in Nevada* https://en.wikipedia.org/wiki/Mark_Twain_in_Nevada
- *The Celebrated Jumping Frog of Calaveras County* https://www.britannica.com/topic/The-Celebrated-Jumping-Frog-of-Calaveras-County
- *Satire and Irony in Mark Twain's Works* https://literaryodyssey.com/blog/a-complete-exploration-of-satire-and-irony-in-mark-twain-s-works

- *"Huck Finn's Literary Dialect" by Ann C. Reed - BearWorks* https://bearworks.missouristate.edu/theses/331/
- *Writing "Huck Finn": Mark Twain's Creative Process* https://www.jstor.org/stable/j.ctt3fht8q
- *Theater and the Popularity of the Deadpan Style* https://publishing.cdlib.org/ucpressebooks/view?docId=ft4n39n9g5&chunk.id=d0e977&toc.id=&brand=ucpress
- *Political Corruption in Postbellum America* https://opened.cuny.edu/courseware/lesson/410/student-old/?task=2
- *Mark Twain's Inconvenient Truths* https://stanfordmag.org/contents/mark-twain-s-inconvenient truths
- *The secret to Mark Twain's friendship with Nikola Tesla* https://bigthink.com/high-culture/the-secret-to-mark-twains-friendship-with-nikola-tesla/
- *StoryMapJS: The Travels of Mark Twain* https://uploads.knightlab.com/storymapjs/7dfb13e7213681bd04609999e2e46684/the-travels-of-mark-twain/index.html
- *The Adventures of Tom Sawyer Study Guide - Mark Twain* https://www.litcharts.com/lit/the-adventures-of-tom-sawyer
- *Adventures of Huckleberry Finn* https://en.wikipedia.org/wiki/Adventures_of_Huckleberry_Finn
- *A Connecticut Yankee in King Arthur's Court* https://en.wikipedia.org/wiki/A_Connecticut_Yankee_in_King_Arthur%27s_Court
- *Reading Pudd'nhead Wilson: Criticism and Commentary ...* https://scholarlypublishingcollective.org/psup/recep

tion/article/9/1/4/197869/Reading-Pudd-nhead-Wilson-Criticism-and-Commentary

- *The Love Letters of Mark Twain* https://www.theatlantic.com/magazine/archive/1948/01/the-love-letters-of-mark-twain/644011/
- *Mark Twain Loses Money Backing The Paige Compositor* https://www.historyofinformation.com/detail.php?id=4709
- *Mark Twain on a Dumb Sense of Vast Loss* https://www.skmurphy.com/blog/2015/09/20/mark-twain-on-a-dumb-sense-of-vast-loss/
- *Pop Culture Influence - Mark Twain* https://marktwainhouse.org/about/mark-twain/pop-culture-influence/
- *Mark Twain and William Dean Howells: the friendship that ...* https://www.loa.org/news-and-views/981-mark-twain-and-william-dean-howells-the-friendship-that-transformed-american-literature/
- *The Bret Harte-Mark Twain Feud: An Inside Narrative* https://www.jstor.org/stable/41641376
- *Chapter 33 - Copyright, Trademark, and Brand* https://www.cambridge.org/core/books/mark-twain-in-context/copyright-trademark-and-brand/3B4A4F911079E5E8CDF8176D497122F0
- *An Interview with Mark Twain - Story of the Week* https://storyoftheweek.loa.org/2019/04/an-interview-with-mark-twain.html
- *Controversy at Cherry Hill - Huck Finn Teachers Guide* https://www.pbs.org/wgbh/cultureshock/teachers/huck/controversy.html
- *Mark Twain and Critical Race Theory* https://www.insidehighered.com/views/2021/10/07/

mark-twain-was-american-lits-first-critical-race-theorist-opinion
- *Chapter 32 - Film, Television, and Theater Adaptations*
  https://www.cambridge.org/core/books/mark-twain-in-context/film-television-and-theater-adaptations/AACD159AC5BFF68FD492DC922270DE32
- *Mark Twain - Humorist, Novelist, Satirist*
  https://www.britannica.com/biography/Mark-Twain/Reputation-and-legacy

www.ingramcontent.com/pod-product-compliance
Lightning Source LLC
Chambersburg PA
CBHW051500050726

47593CB00005B/2162